Reader's Digest
Modern
Meat
Classics

Reader's Digest

Modern
Meat
Classics

Published by The Reader's Digest Association Limited
London • New York • Sydney • Montreal

Modern Meat Classics is part of a series of cookery books called
Eat Well Live Well and was created by Amazon Publishing Limited.
It was formerly published in hardback under the title **Meat Classics**.

Series Editor *Norma MacMillan*
Volume Editor *Jeni Wright*
Art Director *Ruth Prentice*
Photographic Direction *Ruth Prentice, Alison Shackleton*
DTP *Peter Howard*
Editorial Assistant *Jasmine Brown*
Nutritionists *Moya de Wet, BSc Hons (Nutri.), A. Dip. Dietetics,
Fiona Hunter, BSc Hons (Nutri.), Dip. Dietetics*

Contributors
Writers *Shirley Bond, Sara Buenfeld, Carole Clements,
Linda Collister, Beverly LeBlanc, Sara Lewis, Maggie Mayhew,
Kate Moseley, Maggie Pannell, Marlena Spieler*
Recipe Testers *Pat Alburey, Catherine Atkinson,
Valerie Barrett, Anna Brandenburger, Emma-Lee Gow,
Clare Lewis, Gina Steer, Susanna Tee*
Photographers *Martin Brigdale, Gus Filgate, William Lingwood, Sean Myers*
Stylist *Helen Trent*
Home Economists *Joanna Farrow, Lucy McKelvie, Bridget Sargeson,
Linda Tubby, Sunil Vijayakar*

For Reader's Digest
Series Editor *Rachel Warren Chadd*
Production Controllers *Kathy Brown, Jane Holyer*

Reader's Digest General Books
Editorial Director *Cortina Butler*
Art Director *Nick Clark*

Paperback edition 2004
Paperback Art Editor *Jane McKenna*

ISBN 0 276 42888 9

First Edition Copyright © 2000
The Reader's Digest Association Limited
11 Westferry Circus, Canary Wharf, London E14 4HE

Copyright © 2000 Reader's Digest Association Far East Limited
Philippines copyright © 2000 Reader's Digest Association Far East Limited

We are committed to both the quality of our products and the service we provide
to our customers. We value your comments, so please feel free to contact us on
08705 113366, or via our web site at www.readersdigest.co.uk
If you have any comments about the content of our books, you can contact
us at: gbeditorial@readersdigest.co.uk

Notes for the reader
• Use all metric or all imperial measures when preparing a recipe,
as the two sets of measurements are not exact equivalents.
• Recipes were tested using metric measures and conventional
(not fan-assisted) ovens. Medium eggs were used, unless
otherwise specified.
• Can sizes are approximate, as weights can vary slightly
according to the manufacturer.
• Preparation and cooking times are only intended as a guide.

The nutritional information in this book is for reference only.
The editors urge anyone with continuing medical problems or
symptoms to consult a doctor.

Contents

Eating well to live well

Eating a healthy diet can help you look good, feel great and have lots of energy. Nutrition fads come and go, but the simple keys to eating well remain the same: enjoy a variety of food – no single food contains all the vitamins, minerals, fibre and other essential components you need for health and vitality – and get the balance right by looking at the proportions of the different foods you eat. Add some regular exercise too – at least 30 minutes a day, 3 times a week – and you'll be helping yourself to live well and make the most of your true potential.

Getting it into proportion

Current guidelines are that most people in the UK should eat more starchy foods, more fruit and vegetables, and less fat, meat products and sugary foods. It is almost impossible to give exact amounts that you should eat, as every single person's requirements vary, depending on size, age and the amount of energy expended during the day. However, nutrition experts have suggested an ideal balance of the different foods that provide us with energy (calories) and the nutrients needed for health. The number of daily portions of each of the food groups will vary from person to person – for example, an active teenager might need to eat up to 14 portions of starchy carbohydrates every day, whereas a sedentary adult would only require 6 or 7 portions – but the proportions of the food groups in relation to each other should ideally stay the same.

More detailed explanations of food groups and nutritional terms can be found on pages 156–158, together with brief guidelines on amounts which can be used in conjunction with the nutritional analyses of the recipes. A simple way to get the balance right, however, is to imagine a daily 'plate' divided into the different food groups. On the imaginary 'plate', starchy carbohydrates fill at least one-third of the space, thus constituting the main part of your meals. Fruit and vegetables fill the same amount of space. The remaining third of the 'plate' is divided mainly between protein foods and dairy foods, with just a little space allowed for foods containing fat and sugar. These are the proportions to aim for.

It isn't essential to eat the ideal proportions on the 'plate' at every meal, or even every day – balancing them over a week or two is just as good. The healthiest diet for you and your family is one that is generally balanced and sustainable in the long term.

Our daily plate

Starchy carbohydrate foods: eat 6–14 portions a day
At least 50% of the calories in a healthy diet should come from carbohydrates, and most of that from starchy foods – bread, potatoes and other starchy vegetables, pasta, rice and cereals. For most people in the UK this means doubling current intake. Starchy carbohydrates are the best foods for energy. They also provide protein and essential vitamins and minerals, particularly those from the B group. Eat a variety of starchy foods, choosing wholemeal or wholegrain types whenever possible, because the fibre they contain helps to prevent constipation, bowel disease, heart disease and other health problems.
What is a portion of starchy foods?
Some examples are: 3 tbsp breakfast cereal • 2 tbsp muesli • 1 slice of bread or toast • 1 bread roll, bap or bun • 1 small pitta bread, naan bread or chapatti • 3 crackers or crispbreads • 1 medium-sized potato • 1 medium-sized plantain or small sweet potato • 2 heaped tbsp boiled rice • 2 heaped tbsp boiled pasta.

Fruit and vegetables: eat at least 5 portions a day
Nutrition experts are unanimous that we would all benefit from eating more fruit and vegetables each day – a total of at least 400 g (14 oz) of fruit and vegetables (edible part) is the target. Fruit and vegetables provide vitamin C for immunity and healing, and other 'antioxidant' vitamins and minerals for protection against cardiovascular disease and cancer. They also offer several 'phytochemicals' that help protect against cancer, and B vitamins, especially folate, which is important for women planning a pregnancy, to prevent birth defects. All of these, plus other nutrients, work together to boost well-being.

Antioxidant nutrients (e.g. vitamins C and beta-carotene, which are mainly derived from fruit and vegetables) and vitamin E help to prevent harmful free radicals in the body initiating or accelerating cancer, heart disease, cataracts, arthritis, general ageing, sun damage to skin, and damage to sperm. Free radicals occur naturally as a by-product of normal cell function, but are also caused by pollutants such as tobacco smoke and over-exposure to sunlight.
What is a portion of fruit or vegetables?
Some examples are: 1 medium-sized portion of vegetables or salad • 1 medium-sized piece of fresh fruit • 6 tbsp (about 140 g/5 oz) stewed or canned fruit • 1 small glass (100 ml/3½ fl oz) fruit juice.

Dairy foods: eat 2–3 portions a day
Dairy foods, such as milk, cheese, yogurt and fromage frais, are the best source of calcium for strong bones and teeth, and important for the nervous system. They also provide some protein for growth and repair, vitamin B_{12}, and vitamin A for healthy eyes. They are particularly valuable foods for young children, who need full-fat versions at least up to age 2. Dairy foods are also especially important for adolescent girls to prevent the development of osteoporosis later in life, and for women throughout life generally.

To limit fat intake, wherever possible adults should choose lower-fat dairy foods, such as semi-skimmed milk and low-fat yogurt.
What is a portion of dairy foods?
Some examples are: 1 medium-sized glass (200 ml/7 fl oz) milk • 1 matchbox-sized piece (40 g/1½ oz) Cheddar cheese • 1 small pot of yogurt • 125 g (4½ oz) cottage cheese or fromage frais.

Protein foods: eat 2–4 portions a day

Lean meat, fish, eggs and vegetarian alternatives provide protein for growth and cell repair, as well as iron to prevent anaemia. Meat also provides B vitamins for healthy nerves and digestion, especially vitamin B_{12}, and zinc for growth and healthy bones and skin. Only moderate amounts of these protein-rich foods are required. An adult woman needs about 45 g of protein a day and an adult man 55 g, which constitutes about 11% of a day's calories. This is less than the current average intake. For optimum health, we need to eat some protein every day.

What is a portion of protein-rich food?

Some examples are: 3 slices (85–100 g/3–3½ oz) of roast beef, pork, ham, lamb or chicken • about 100 g (3½ oz) grilled offal • 115–140 g (4–5 oz) cooked fillet of white or oily fish (not fried in batter) • 3 fish fingers • 2 eggs (up to 7 a week) • about 140 g/5 oz baked beans • 60 g (2¼ oz) nuts, peanut butter or other nut products.

Foods containing fat: 1–5 portions a day

Unlike fruit, vegetables and starchy carbohydrates, which can be eaten in abundance, fatty foods should not exceed 33% of the day's calories in a balanced diet, and only 10% of this should be from saturated fat. This quantity of fat may seem a lot, but it isn't – fat contains more than twice as many calories per gram as either carbohydrate or protein.

Overconsumption of fat is a major cause of weight and health problems. A healthy diet must contain a certain amount of fat to provide fat-soluble vitamins and essential fatty acids, needed for the development and function of the brain, eyes and nervous system, but we only need a small amount each day – just 25 g is required, which is much less than we consume in our Western diet. The current recommendations from the Department of Health are a maximum of 71 g fat (of this, 21.5 g saturated) for women each day and 93.5 g fat (28.5 g saturated) for men. The best sources of the essential fatty acids are natural fish oils and pure vegetable oils.

What is a portion of fatty foods?

Some examples are: 1 tsp butter or margarine • 2 tsp low-fat spread • 1 tsp cooking oil • 1 tbsp mayonnaise or vinaigrette (salad dressing) • 1 tbsp cream • 1 individual packet of crisps.

Foods containing sugar: 0–2 portions a day

Although many foods naturally contain sugars (e.g. fruit contains fructose, milk lactose), health experts recommend that we limit 'added' sugars. Added sugars, such as table sugar, provide only calories – they contain no vitamins, minerals or fibre to contribute to health, and it is not necessary to eat them at all. But, as the old adage goes, 'a little of what you fancy does you good' and sugar is no exception. Denial of foods, or using them as rewards or punishment, is not a healthy attitude to eating, and can lead to cravings, binges and yo-yo dieting. Sweet foods are a pleasurable part of a well-balanced diet, but added sugars should account for no more than 11% of the total daily carbohydrate intake.

In assessing how much sugar you consume, don't forget that it is a major ingredient of many processed and ready-prepared foods.

What is a portion of sugary foods?

Some examples are: 3 tsp sugar • 1 heaped tsp jam or honey • 2 biscuits • half a slice of cake • 1 doughnut • 1 Danish pastry • 1 small bar of chocolate • 1 small tube or bag of sweets.

Too salty

Salt (sodium chloride) is essential for a variety of body functions, but we tend to eat too much through consumption of salty processed foods, 'fast' foods and ready-prepared foods, and by adding salt in cooking and at the table. The end result can be rising blood pressure as we get older, which puts us at higher risk of heart disease and stroke. Eating more vegetables and fruit increases potassium intake, which can help to counteract the damaging effects of salt.

Alcohol in a healthy diet

In recent research, moderate drinking of alcohol has been linked with a reduced risk of heart disease and stroke among men and women over 45. However, because of other risks associated with alcohol, particularly in excessive quantities, no doctor would recommend taking up drinking if you are teetotal. The healthiest pattern of drinking is to enjoy small amounts of alcohol with food, to have alcohol-free days and always to avoid getting drunk. A well-balanced diet is vital because nutrients from food (vitamins and minerals) are needed to detoxify the alcohol.

Water – the best choice

Drinking plenty of non-alcoholic liquid each day is an often overlooked part of a well-balanced diet. A minimum of 8 glasses (which is about 2 litres/3½ pints) is the ideal. If possible, these should not all be tea or coffee, as these are stimulants and diuretics, which cause the body to lose liquids, taking with them water-soluble vitamins. Water is the best choice. Other good choices are fruit or herb teas or tisanes, fruit juices – diluted with water, if preferred – or semi-skimmed milk (full-fat milk for very young children). Fizzy sugary or acidic drinks such as cola are more likely to damage tooth enamel than other drinks.

As a guide to the vitamin and mineral content of foods and recipes in the book, we have used the following terms and symbols, based on the percentage of the daily RNI provided by one serving for the average adult man or woman aged 19–49 years (see also pages 156–158):

✓✓✓ *or* excellent   at least 50% (half)

✓✓   *or* good   25–50% (one-quarter to one-half)

✓   *or* useful   10–25% (one-tenth to one-quarter)

Note that recipes contribute other nutrients, but the analyses only include those that provide at least 10% RNI per portion. Vitamins and minerals where deficiencies are rare are not included.

Mighty Meat

Wonderfully nutritious and versatile

Meat is good for you in so many ways. It provides an
excellent concentrated source of protein as well as
offering many valuable nutrients. From the cook's point
of view, meat is amazingly versatile – the wide variety of
interesting cuts can be prepared and cooked in myriad
ways to suit any occasion, budget or time available, and
will provide a huge range of wonderful flavours and
different textures. To add to the choice, there are lean
venison and tasty wild boar, both becoming more widely
available, plus more unusual meats
such as ostrich, and savoury
preserved and processed meats.
All of these can be enjoyed as part
of a healthy, well-balanced diet.

Meat in a healthy diet

Meat provides many of the essential nutrients we need for good health and well-being, in a delicious and satisfying form. It is an excellent source of vital protein, and also offers an abundance of vitamins and minerals. It can be healthily lean too, with some cuts containing no more fat than chicken or turkey.

Protein – the body builder

Everyone needs protein, to grow and build up strength, to continually replenish body tissues, and to maintain good health. Every part of our bodies – muscles, bones, skin, hair and nails – depends on it. To fulfil this important role, an adult woman needs about 45 g protein daily, while an adult man needs 55 g. Eating meat is an excellent way to obtain the protein we require.

Although a regular protein intake is needed for optimum health, the daily requirement isn't really very much, and most of us eat far more than this. In fact, on a healthy well-balanced 'plate', protein foods should occupy only about one-sixth of the space – the largest part of the plate should be filled with starchy carbohydrates and fruit and vegetables. This turns traditional meal planning of 'meat with 2 veg' on its head – meat and other protein foods should be just one of the many component parts of a meal, not the major part of it.

Vital vitamins

A regular intake of vitamins is essential for good health. Meat provides many of them.
- Vitamin A is required for growth and normal development; it also protects against infection, and aids healthy skin, eyes and night vision. The active form of vitamin A, retinol, is found in meat, especially liver and other offal. Retinol is readily absorbed and used by the body.
- Vitamin D, combined with calcium, works to keep bones and teeth strong and healthy. Red meat is one of the richest natural sources of vitamin D in the diet.
- B vitamins are vital for all cell function in the body, but especially for healthy nerve and blood cells. Meat supplies most of the eight vitamins in the group. Of special importance is B_{12}, as foods of animal origin are the principal dietary source.

A comparison of the protein content of 100 g (3½ oz) boneless lean meat with other protein foods

beef		veal	
fillet steak, grilled	29 g	escalope, pan-fried	33 g
mince, cooked	25 g		
sirloin, roasted	32 g	**venison**	
		roasted	36 g
lamb			
cutlets, grilled	28 g	**other protein foods**	
leg, roasted	31 g	Cheddar cheese	25.5 g
loin chops, grilled	29 g	chicken breast, roasted	25 g
		cod fillet, baked	21 g
pork		eggs (2), poached	12.5 g
fillet, grilled	33 g	lentils, boiled	8.8 g
leg, roasted	35 g	red kidney beans, boiled	8.4 g
loin chop, grilled	32 g	tofu, uncooked	8.1 g

Essential minerals

Meat supplies many minerals, in particular iron and zinc.
- Iron is essential for the formation of the red blood cells that carry oxygen around the body – iron deficiency causes tiredness and anaemia. Women and teenage girls are prone to anaemia if their bodies do not absorb enough iron to cover losses of blood during menstruation and childbirth. Eating red meat makes a valuable contribution to the iron we need.
- Zinc is vital for normal growth and the healthy functioning of the immune and reproductive systems. It is also important for healthy skin, especially where skin healing is necessary. Among the best sources of zinc are red meat (beef and lamb in

▲ A healthy portion of meat on a well-balanced 'plate' is deliciously satisfying when roast potatoes and root vegetables, freshly cooked greens and a tasty gravy are served alongside. Pictured above is Sunday special roast beef (see page 98)

particular) and liver. Zinc is also found in wholegrain cereals, such as wholemeal bread, but the zinc in meat is more readily absorbed by the body. To make the maximum amount of zinc available, combine meat and cereals in the same meal. A good example of this is spaghetti bolognese – meat is in the sauce and cereal (wheat) is in the pasta.

Iron – a question of absorption

Much of the iron we eat is not properly or completely absorbed by our bodies. This is particularly true of the iron found in plant foods, which need to be eaten with vitamin-C rich fruits and vegetables in order for iron absorption to be maximised. The iron found in meat is a different kind. Called haem iron, it is easily absorbed by the body, and does not need to be combined with other foods.

• Meat also supplies three microminerals: copper and phosphorus, needed for a healthy respiratory tract and healthy bones, and selenium, which acts as an antioxidant. Only tiny amounts of these are required to help maintain good health.

What about vegetarians?

A properly balanced vegetarian diet is very healthy, but some people (young girls in particular) stop eating meat and eat only the salad or vegetables in a meal, so missing out on many vital nutrients. Others may eat too much cheese as a substitute for meat, not realising that the fat content can be very high. Sufficient protein and other essential nutrients can be obtained from combinations of pulses, cereals, vegetables, fruits and nuts, and you need to know about these if you have a vegetarian in the family. Vegans, who eat no animal products, need to eat some foods fortified with vitamin B_{12}, to be sure of not missing out on this vital nutrient.

mighty meat

11

Making the best choice

Meat in all its variety – beef joints, pork fillets, lamb chops, steaks, mince and the different kinds of offal – is an important part of a healthy well-balanced diet. As a first-class protein food, we don't need to eat a lot of it, so it makes sense to select the best we can afford, and the leanest choice available.

A healthy variety

All the main kinds of meat – beef, veal, lamb and pork – are excellent sources of protein. They also provide the same vitamins and minerals, although in slightly differing amounts. For example, although all red meat is rich in B vitamins, pork, ham and bacon are especially rich in vitamin B_1, and beef is rich in B_{12}. So it's best to eat a variety of different meats to be sure you derive the maximum nutritional benefits on offer.

The fat issue

Despite its positive contribution to the diet, meat is often criticised for its fat content. Saturated fat in particular has given meat a bad name, and this has caused some people to consider omitting meat from their diets altogether. In fact, only about half of the fat in meat is saturated – much less than it used to be, thanks to modern breeding techniques. The

Animal welfare and consumer choice

In the UK, comprehensive guidelines, backed by legislation, control animal welfare and all procedures throughout the food chain, including meat production. But in response to consumer demand, farm assurance schemes, such as the RSPCA's Freedom Food Standards, have been established, specifically to safeguard animal welfare, and food produced under these schemes is clearly labelled. Organic meat, from farms where the routine use of antibiotics is prohibited and the content of animal feed is rigorously controlled, is becoming more popular, and many other farms are changing to outdoor 'free-range' production instead of indoor intensive-rearing systems. When choosing meat, read the label or ask the butcher about the supplier, bearing in mind that all meat is equally nutritious.

▲ Lean minced beef is low in fat and yet rich in zinc, iron and vitamins B and D. Beefburgers with beetroot relish (see page 80) are a delicious and healthy way to prepare these family favourites

▲ Lamb provides lots of B vitamins, zinc and iron. In Aromatic spiced lamb cutlets (see page 32) it is marinated and grilled, then served with an apricot and almond coucous, a great source of starchy carbohydrate

remaining fat content is unsaturated – primarily the monounsaturated kind with a little polyunsaturated.

Fat is very high in calories – twice as many per gram as either carbohydrate or protein – and overconsumption of saturated fat is a major cause of health concerns, such as weight problems, coronary heart disease and some cancers. This is why nutrition experts recommend that we reduce the total amount of fatty foods we eat. According to current Department of Health guidelines, only 33% of our total daily calories should come from fat (of any kind), and of that a maximum of 10% should be from saturated fat. For an adult woman this means a daily maximum amount of 71 g fat, of which 21.5 g can be saturated; for an adult man the daily amount is 93.5 g fat, of which 28.5 g can be saturated.

Eating moderate portions of lean meat can help to keep fat intake within healthy limits, while still providing all the benefits that meat has to offer.

Cutting along the seam

Seam butchery is a technique of butchering that reduces the amount of fat in meat. It involves the removal of individual muscles by following the seams in the carcass. As a result, any visible fat between the seams can be cut away and discarded before sale to produce very lean, boneless cuts. These are ready-trimmed and portioned for immediate use.

Fat content of 100 g (3½ oz) boneless lean meat*

	Total fat	Saturates	Mono-unsaturates	Poly-unsaturates
beef				
mince, lean	9.6 g	4.2 g	0.4 g	0.4 g
rump steak	4.1 g	1.7 g	1.7 g	0.3 g
sirloin	4.5 g	2.0 g	1.9 g	0.2 g
topside	2.7 g	1.1 g	1.2 g	0.2 g
lamb				
leg	8.3 g	3.8 g	3.2 g	0.4 g
pork				
leg	2.2 g	0.9 g	0.9 g	0.4 g
loin steaks	3.4 g	1.2 g	1.3 g	0.6 g
venison				
average	1.6 g	0.8 g	0.4 g	0.4 g

* The total fat figure includes fatty compounds and other fatty acids in addition to saturates and mono and polyunsaturates.

▲ Liver is rich in iron and vitamins A, B and D, and eating it just once a week can be beneficial. Calf's liver with rigatoni, broccoli and orange (see page 128) is a superb way to serve it

▲ Venison has twice as much iron as beef, and it is a good source of vitamins and minerals. It is also very low in fat. Try it in Venison and chestnut casserole (see page 120), with mash and roasted vegetables

The big four

Beef, veal, lamb and pork, and their offal, are excellent sources of protein, and they provide many other essential nutrients. Each meat has its own distinctive flavours and textures, and offers a wonderful variety of cuts. With healthy methods of preparing and cooking the different cuts, you can bring out their best points.

boneless sirloin joint

Beef

Beef comes from steers or bullocks reared to 18 months old or from heifers not required for breeding. The meat should be open-grained and moist with a good red colour. If it is a darker, reddish-brown, it will have been hung or aged for at least 2–3 weeks and will have a fuller, 'beefier' flavour.

Beef is both an excellent source of zinc and a useful source of iron. It also provides vitamins from the B group (particularly B_{12}) and is a useful source of vitamin D.

- Sirloin, foreribs, topside and thick flank (top rump) are the traditional beef joints for roasting. Lean and tender fillet can also be roasted, either whole or cut into smaller joints. When

rump steak

buying a boneless joint allow 100–170 g (3½–6 oz) per person, or 225–340 g (8–12 oz) for meat on the bone. These raw weights allow for any waste in preparation and for loss of weight during cooking. An average cooked portion size is 85–100 g (3–3½ oz).

- Brisket and silverside are joints that become tender and succulent with long, slow cooking, so they are ideal for a pot roast – cooked in one large piece in a casserole with liquid, vegetables and flavourings.
- Sirloin, rump and fillet steaks are tender enough for quick cooking methods such as grilling, griddling, barbecuing and frying. Grilling is the healthiest way to cook steaks, as no extra fat is needed. Griddling on a ridged cast-iron grill pan or a heavy-based non-stick frying pan is almost as good, as long as you use the minimum amount of an oil such as olive or

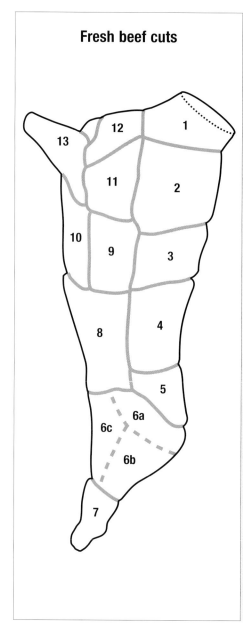

Fresh beef cuts

1. neck
2. chuck, including blade
3. forerib
4. sirloin, including fillet (joint and steak)
5. rump (rump steak and skirt)
6. round:
   (a) topside
   (b) silverside
   (c) thick flank or top rump
7. leg
8. flank
9. thin rib
10. brisket
11. top or thick rib
12. clod
13. shin

cubed chuck steak

sunflower. A good tip is to get the pan hot before you put the meat on to cook. Steak can also be cut into cubes for kebabs – rump steak is particularly good because it is firm and will stay on the skewers while cooking – or into strips for stir-fries.

● Shin, leg, neck and clod (from the neck) are tougher cuts, being muscular or weight-bearing in the animal, so they need long, gentle stewing to make them tender. There is no limit to the different vegetables, herbs and spices that can be used in meaty stews to provide delicious flavour combinations, and the slow cooking allows plenty of time for the meat to become beautifully tender.

● Back or thick ribs, chuck and blade, sold as 'braising steak', are not as tough as stewing cuts such as shin, but too tough for grilling or griddling. They are ideal for stews and casseroles.

Veal

loin joint

Veal is the meat of a young calf 18–20 weeks old. It should be a very pale cream or delicate pink colour with virtually no fat. This leanness is good from the nutritional point of view, but it does mean that some recipes for veal need to incorporate a liquid or sauce to make them more moist and juicy.

Veal has a very similar nutritional profile to beef, although it provides only about half the amount of iron.

● Leg is a prime lean cut for roasting – allow 225 g (8 oz) per person when buying meat on the bone. A boned and stuffed leg is even better, because the stuffing helps to make the meat moist and tasty.

escalopes

● Fillet and topside, both cut from the leg, can be roasted successfully as joints, but are often cut into slices across the grain and beaten thin to make escalopes and schnitzels.

● Rump is usually cut into medallions or escalopes. Being thin cuts, these are perfect for very quick pan-frying.

● Loin makes an excellent roasting joint on the bone, or boned, stuffed and rolled. Chops and cutlets are lean and tender, and can be roasted, grilled, pan-fried or braised.

● Shoulder, when boned and stuffed, makes a good roasting cut, but the meat is more usually removed from the bone, trimmed of fat and cut into cubes for use in pies and stews. With long, gentle cooking it becomes very tender.

● Shin, from the legs, is good in stews, the best known being the Italian osso buco.

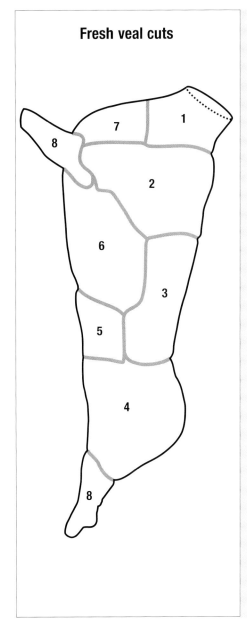

Fresh veal cuts

1. neck
2. shoulder or chuck
3. loin (joint, chops and cutlets)
4. leg, including rump, fillet and topside
5. thick flank
6. breast
7. clod
8. shin or knuckle

leg

Lamb

Of all the red meats, lamb is the one that has benefited the most from the new cutting and preparation techniques. More fat is now removed from the meat before being sold, and prepared new cuts are ideal for quick meals for one or two people. Early in the season, the meat from young lambs is a paler pink than that of older animals and it has a finer grain.

Lamb is an excellent source of vitamin B_{12} and zinc, a good source of vitamin B_1 (thiamin) and a useful source of iron.

• Leg, loin, best end of neck and shoulder are all excellent joints for traditional roasts on the bone. The leg can also be boned and 'butterflied', or opened out flat, and then grilled or

chump and cutlets

barbecued. Loin is often boned, stuffed and rolled for roasting – many shops sell it ready-prepared. Best end of neck can be roasted as a whole rack of 6–7 cutlets or, for a special occasion, two racks can be joined, either as a guard of honour or a crown roast. Most butchers prepare these to order, and will stuff the centre of a crown roast if you like, although you may prefer your own stuffing. Allow 85–170 g (3–6 oz) per person when buying boneless meat and 225–340 g (8–12 oz) if the meat is on the bone.

• Neck fillet, best end of neck cutlets, steaks cut from the top of the leg, and chump, loin and double loin chops are all excellent for grilling. The same cuts can also be cooked on a ridged cast-iron grill pan or in a non-stick frying pan using a little oil. Loin and chump chops are also good for roasting, as are lamb steaks, either on or off the bone. Lean and tender neck fillet and boneless leg steaks are perfect cut into cubes for kebabs or thin strips for stir-fries. If they are marinated before cooking, the meat will be extra succulent and tasty.

Fresh lamb cuts

1. neck and scrag
2. shoulder and middle neck (neck fillet)
3. rib or best end of neck (rack, crown roast and cutlets)
4. loin (joint and chops)
5. chump (chops)
6. leg (joint and steaks)
7. breast

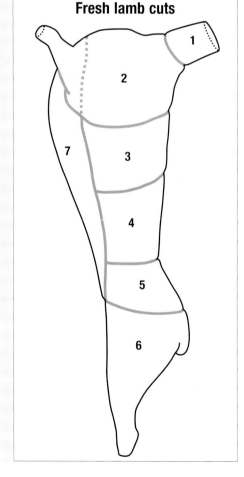

boneless loin joint

Pork

The meat of the pig is sold fresh as pork, used in fresh meat products such as sausages, preserved as bacon and ham and in salami-type sausages, and used cooked in pies. Due to modern selective breeding techniques, pork is now leaner than it used to be – there is less fat within the tissues of the meat and the layer of back fat is very thin – which makes it a very healthy choice. Fresh pork should be smooth and pink, not at all grey or damp-looking.

Pork is an excellent source of vitamin B_{12} and a good source of zinc and vitamins B_1 (thiamin) and B_6.

• Leg, shoulder (hand and spring) and loin are the most popular lean cuts for roasting. Any fat on the joint can be removed before cooking or left on so it bastes the meat during roasting – stand the joint on a rack in the roasting tin so the fat drips through. The skin on a pork joint will also help to keep the meat moist during roasting, but it's best not to eat too

fillet

much of the crisp crackling that forms as it is very high in saturated fat – 45 g fat in every 100 g (3½ oz) of crackling. (The skin should not be left on when moist cooking methods such as casseroling and stewing are used, or the fat underneath it will melt into the cooking liquid.) Leg and loin can also be boned and stuffed before roasting. For a boneless roasting joint, allow 85–170 g (3–6 oz) per person; for a joint on the bone, allow 225–340 g (8–12 oz).

● Fillet, also called tenderloin, is very lean and tender, as its name suggests. It can be roasted whole, but it is most often cut into thin slices or strips for pan-fries and stir-fries, and into cubes for casseroles and kebabs.

● Loin and chump chops can be roasted, or they can be grilled or pan-fried. The meat is lean and can dry out easily, so it is a good idea to coat it with a glaze or baste it during cooking, or use a moist cooking method such as braising. Loin chops may include the kidney, which adds extra flavour and more iron.

● Leg and shoulder (hand and spring) make good pot roasts, ending up deliciously moist and tender.

Nutrient-rich offal

Offal includes liver, kidneys, heart, tongue, sweetbreads, brains and trotters. Liver and kidneys are still popular, but other types of offal are not as widely eaten as they used to be, although they can be delicious. All offal is very nutritious, but liver, heart and kidneys are the stars, rich in iron and B vitamins, especially B_3 and B_{12}, and vitamins A and D. As vitamins A and D can be stored in the body, just one 85 g (3 oz) serving of offal once a week will build up and restore stocks. If you're not too keen on offal, you can combine it with other meats, say in a steak and kidney pie or in a pâté.

● Calf's liver is very tender and delicate in flavour. It is best pan-fried, stir-fried or grilled. Lamb's liver has a fairly strong flavour. It, too, can be grilled, but is better used in a casserole or stew. Pig's liver has the strongest flavour of all and a soft texture. Although it is suitable for casseroles, it is the favourite for pâtés and terrines.

● Lamb's kidneys are small and tender with a good flavour. They can be grilled or fried. Allow 2 kidneys per portion. Ox, calf's and pig's kidneys have a stronger flavour and are good in casseroles and stews. Allow 1 or 2 per person, depending on size.

● Whole ox heart is good stuffed and roasted, and it can also be sliced and cooked in stews and casseroles. Lamb's heart is more tender than calf's, but both can be stuffed and braised or roasted.

● Tongue may be pickled before cooking and pressing. Small lamb's tongues can be pressed together in a casserole, or they can be sliced and served cold.

● Fried calf's and lamb's sweetbreads are a traditional delicacy. Ox sweetbreads are tougher, and are best used in stews and stuffings.

● Calf's brains are considered to be the best and are traditionally served poached with a sauce. Lamb's brains are usually used in stews.

● Trotters are the feet of pigs or sheep. They can be boiled or grilled for eating hot, or simmered in a stock to help set it for an aspic.

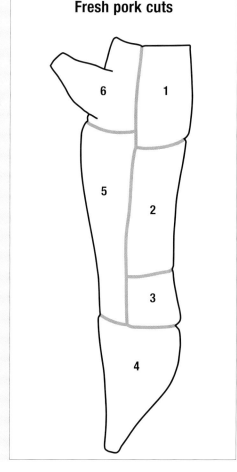

Fresh pork cuts

1. spare rib (joint and chops)
2. loin, including fillet or tenderloin (joint and chops)
3. chump (joint and chops)
4. leg
5. belly
6. shoulder or hand and spring

Ring the changes

Apart from beef, veal, lamb and pork, there are many other types of meat that add variety to everyday meals and special occasions. Preserved and processed meats are packed with flavour, so a little goes a long way, while meats like venison and buffalo are exceptionally low in fat and so make a great addition to a healthy diet.

Ever-popular bangers

Individual butchers make their own fresh sausages according to traditional recipes, and these vary from one part of the country to another, but the content is regulated and the type of meat and the percentage of it must be declared, with details of any preservatives, additives and flavourings used. To be sure of what you are buying, read the labels on the packets, or information displayed in the butcher's cabinet, paying particular attention to the fat content. Sausages with a high meat content are the best healthy choice.

Pork and beef are the most common meats used for sausages, but lamb, venison, wild boar, chicken and other speciality sausages are also available. The best low-fat cooking methods are grilling, barbecuing and baking on a rack in the oven, but sausages can also be cooked on a ridged cast-iron grill pan or in a non-stick frying pan. They are very good in casseroles and stews, and chopped up in sauces for pasta.

An ABC of special sausages

There is a wonderful variety of sausages from all parts of the world, many of them with unusual and exciting flavours. Each country has its own specialities, some of which need cooking and others not.

● Black pudding (*boudin noir* in French) is made from pig's blood (sheep's blood in Scotland), fat, cereals such as oatmeal, and flavourings. It is usually sliced and shallow-fried, grilled or baked.

● Bratwurst is a German smoked sausage made from pork or veal. It is usually grilled or fried.

● Chorizo is a Spanish pork sausage. There are both smoked and unsmoked varieties, and they may be spicy hot. Some can be sliced and eaten raw while others require cooking. A small quantity of chorizo will add lots of flavour to a stew or sauce.

● Frankfurters are long, slim smoked sausages made from a mixture of beef and pork. They can be heated in hot water, grilled or lightly fried, or added to casseroles.

● Salamis of innumerable kinds come from all over Europe. Most are made from pork, but some are a mixture of meats. All are 'matured' for at least a few weeks, which dries them out, and most are ready to eat.

● Toulouse sausages, made from coarsely chopped pork, are an essential ingredient of a traditional French cassoulet.

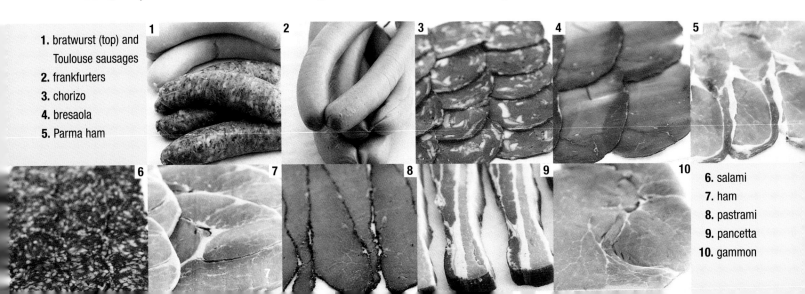

1. bratwurst (top) and Toulouse sausages
2. frankfurters
3. chorizo
4. bresaola
5. Parma ham
6. salami
7. ham
8. pastrami
9. pancetta
10. gammon

Cured for flavour

When meat is preserved by air-drying, salting, smoking or steeping in brine, it is described as 'cured'. Such meat is deliciously savoury, but it is often high in salt and saturated fat, so it is best not to eat too much of it too often. For some of the curing processes, preservatives such as sodium nitrate are used, which can be converted into undesirable nitrites in the body. To counteract the nitrites' effect, it is a good idea to eat cured meats with plenty of vitamin C-rich fruits and vegetables.

• Bacon is the cured meat from the back or side of the pig and may be unsmoked ('green') or smoked. Different smoking methods provide a variety of flavours. Rashers of back bacon are much leaner than streaky.

• Bresaola is cured raw beef from Italy. It is sold in wafer-thin slices to be used in antipasti, but it can be chopped and used in salads and other dishes. It has a strong, gamey flavour.

• Most of the corned beef eaten in Britain today is imported canned from Argentina and is compressed cured and cooked beef. It can be served chilled and thinly sliced with a salad or in sandwiches, or chopped and cooked with potato to make corned beef hash.

• Gammon is a type of bacon that is often sold in thick slices or steaks, or as joints. Collar, forehock, prime back, middle gammon and gammon hock are the best gammon joints for boiling or baking.

• Ham is the cured hind leg of the pig. There are many kinds, according to the breed of pig, its diet and type of cure – many flavours can be added during the curing process. Some hams are simply salted, while others are also smoked. York, Suffolk and Bradenham are famous British hams.

• Pancetta is a streaky bacon from Italy, often used chopped in dishes such as spaghetti carbonara, and in sauces, soups and casseroles. It comes smoked or unsmoked.

• Pastrami is brisket of beef cured with sugar, spices and garlic, then smoked. It is served very thinly sliced.

• Prosciutto *crudo* is salted, air-dried ham from Italy. Prosciutto di Parma (Parma ham) is the most famous – and the most expensive. After a long time maturing, it is usually sliced very thinly and served raw, although it can be chopped and used to flavour risottos and sauces for pasta. It can be used as a leaner alternative to bacon rashers.

Something different

Many large supermarkets stock rabbit and venison as do some butchers and game suppliers. You can also get them by mail order. Very unusual meats such as ostrich, kangaroo and buffalo are more often to be found only on restaurant menus, but may well become more widely available in the future. As with all other meats, strict welfare and production methods are enforced for all these speciality meats.

Rabbit Both wild and domesticated rabbits are sold, and the doe meat is said to be the best. The flesh is pale in colour, with a mild flavour. Nutritionally rabbit is similar to beef, except that it has far less zinc. Each rabbit provides 6–8 pieces, which can be roasted or used in casseroles and stews. Rabbit can be used in any chicken recipe.

Hare Hare is similar to rabbit, being jointed in the same way and offering the same nutritional benefits, but it has stronger-tasting, darker flesh. A whole hare can be stuffed and roasted to serve 6–8 people or joints can be used in casseroles or stews.

Venison Venison is very low in fat, and extremely nutritious. It provides more protein than any of the main types of meat, and has twice as much iron as beef. It is also tender and full of flavour. The leg and saddle are the choicest cuts for roasting, and an average joint will serve 8–10 people. Venison is also sold as lean steaks for pan-frying or grilling. Diced venison makes delicious stews, casseroles and game pies. Minced venison can be used in any recipe for minced beef.

Wild boar The lean meat of the wild boar is full of rich flavour. Marinating before cooking helps to make the meat deliciously moist, and also mellows its rather strong taste. It can be used in recipes for pork or venison.

Ostrich Ostrich is a good low-fat source of protein – it contains less saturated fat than other meats. It is now mostly imported and can be bought in a few specialist stores around the country.

Kangaroo A protected species in the wilds of Australia, kangaroo is bred in captivity under strict food standard regulations for home and export sales. Its meat is low in fat, and is an excellent source of iron and zinc. The flavour is similar to hare and the meat is very tender. It can be used in recipes for chicken.

Buffalo A few specialist butchers shops in Britain sell buffalo fillet. It is an excellent source of protein, and is very low in calories and fat compared with beef and chicken. The fillet is best marinated in wine and herbs and then roasted, or cut into steaks and pan-fried.

Bringing out the best in meat

Animals are bred lean and meat is butchered to keep saturated fat to a minimum, which makes meat a healthy choice for today's cook. Shopping with care and then preparing and cooking for the best results can make sure you and your family enjoy all of meat's many nutritional benefits.

Buying for quality

When buying meat, it helps to be an informed shopper.

● Get to know your local independent butcher or the butcher in your supermarket who will prepare meat to suit your own requirements if you don't see exactly what you want on the shelves.

● Choose well-trimmed lean joints and cuts that look fresh and moist and have a good, healthy colour.

● Check the 'use-by' date on packaged meats.

● Many butchers and supermarkets sell ready-prepared meats such as kebabs, beef olives, stir-fry strips and marinated cuts. These are very convenient to use, but be sure to check what is in them before you buy. Read labels carefully, comparing amounts of saturated fat, sodium, preservatives and additives in different products and brands, and opting for the ones that contain the least of these.

● Some stores label meat as 'lean choice' or something similar. It is worth asking what this means exactly, as it may not be as lean as you think.

● Check the fat content of minced or ground beef, and choose the leanest available. Better still, buy lean meat and mince it yourself in a food processor or mincer, or ask the butcher to mince it for you. If a recipe doesn't require fine mince, you can chop good-quality meat with 2 sharp chef's knives to make a coarse, home-made version.

Keeping fat to a minimum

You can reduce the total fat content of a dish with a few simple preparation techniques.

● Before cooking, trim off any visible fat from steaks, chops and cutlets, and from cubes of meat that are to be used in a casserole or stew. For joints that are to be roasted, you may want to leave a thin layer of fat on so that it bastes the meat during cooking, to keep it moist, but be sure to set the joint on a rack in a roasting tin. This way the meat won't be sitting in its own fat during cooking.

● When making casseroles and stews, don't coat the pieces of meat with flour before browning them at the start of cooking because the flour will absorb any excess fat in the dish during cooking. It is better to brown the meat uncoated, then thicken the well-skimmed cooking liquid at the end if necessary.

● After cooking casseroles and stews, be sure to remove any fat from the surface. A bulb baster is the ideal gadget for this, although you can also use a spoon to skim off the fat, or blot it with kitchen paper. Another idea is to drop in a few ice cubes: fat will solidify round them and they can then be lifted out.

● After roasting, drain off and discard all the fat from the roasting tin before using the meat juices to make a gravy or sauce. A gravy strainer or separator, which is a jug with a spout rising from the bottom, is a great help.

● If possible, make casseroles and stews ahead of time and chill them in the fridge overnight. Any fat will rise to the surface and solidify in a layer that can be easily lifted off before the meat dish is reheated for serving.

● You can 'dry-fry' minced or ground meat in a non-stick frying pan without any fat. Turn and break up the meat as it browns, then tip it into a sieve to drain off all the fat that has come out of the meat. Chopped vegetables such as onion, celery and carrot can be dry-fried with the mince too.

For tender results

Lean meat is not self-basting because it does not have fat 'marbled' throughout the flesh, so you need to take care that it doesn't dry out and become tough during cooking.

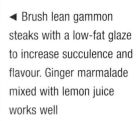

◄ Brush lean gammon steaks with a low-fat glaze to increase succulence and flavour. Ginger marmalade mixed with lemon juice works well

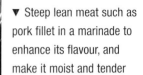

▼ Steep lean meat such as pork fillet in a marinade to enhance its flavour, and make it moist and tender

▲ Add flavour to a joint of lamb by inserting sprigs of fresh rosemary and slivers of garlic into the meat before roasting

◄ Make boneless lean meat go further and boost its nutritional value by adding a tasty stuffing

• If lean cuts such as steaks and escalopes are pounded before cooking, they will cook very quickly and have less time to dry out. Pounding also helps to break down tough fibres and make the meat more tender. To pound raw meat, use a meat mallet or a rolling pin, or the bottom of a saucepan, and cover the meat with cling film or greaseproof paper first, to soften the blow and prevent the meat from tearing.

• You can add moisture and flavour to lean meat and help to tenderise it with a marinade. For tough cuts try including pineapple, figs or papaya in the marinade – these fruits contain enzymes that can have a beneficial tenderising effect on meat. Apricots and prunes have a similar effect, although they do not work quite so well. For best results, leave the meat in its marinade for at least 4 hours, at room temperature.

Punchy flavourings and stuffings

Rather than cooking or serving meat with a rich sauce or gravy, you can add wonderful flavours with herbs, garlic, spices and seasonings, and tasty glazes made from ingredients such as mustard, honey, fruit juice and soy sauce.

Stuffings are an absolute boon for a health-conscious cook. They enhance the flavour of meat and make a moderate amount seem very satisfying, and they can add valuable starchy carbohydrate in the form of bread or rice, plus vitamins, minerals and fibre when vegetables and fruits are included. A stuffing can be pushed inside a joint or a chop, usually in the space left after removing the bone, or you can spread it over boneless meat and then roll the meat up around it. Balls of stuffing can be cooked alongside the meat.

Cooked to perfection

Roasting, grilling, stewing and braising are the traditional cooking methods for meat, and they're still justifiably popular, but cooking on a ridged cast-iron grill pan, barbecuing and stir-frying are fast becoming equal favourites. They use a minimum of fat and they're quick – two great plus points to suit our busy lives today.

Roasting

Roasting is a straightforward method for meat – the joint or other cut is simply cooked uncovered in the oven relatively slowly. The trick is to choose the right cuts, which should be reasonably tender, and to prevent them from drying out so they remain moist and succulent. Here are some useful tips.

● To help keep a boned joint in a good shape and make sure it cooks evenly, tie it with string.

Roasting times and temperatures

The cooking time for roasting meat is based on the weight of the joint, so weigh the meat – after stuffing if there is any – and then calculate the cooking time according to the chart below. The times given are suitable for meat on or off the bone. If you buy one of the special small 'mini-roasts', follow the cooking instructions on the packaging. Also check packet instructions if you are using a roasting bag. The ideal temperature for roasting is 180°C (350°F, gas mark 4). Meat thermometer temperatures are shown in square brackets.

beef and lamb

rare	20 minutes per 450 g (1 lb) plus 20 minutes	[60°C/140°F]
medium	25 minutes per 450 g (1 lb) plus 25 minutes	[70°C/160°F]
well-done	30 minutes per 450 g (1 lb) plus 30 minutes	[80°C/175°F]

veal

well-done	30 minutes per 450 g (1 lb) plus 30 minutes	[80°C/175°F]

pork

medium	30 minutes per 450 g (1 lb) plus 30 minutes	[80°C/175°F]
well-done	35 minutes per 450 g (1 lb) plus 35 minutes	[85°C/180°F]

● Place the meat on a rack in a roasting tin so that the largest cut surfaces of the meat are exposed and any fat is on the top. As the fat melts during roasting it will baste the meat.

● If the meat is very lean, baste it with the hot fat in the roasting tin from time to time during cooking. Alternatively, cover the joint with foil or cook it in a roasting bag. Better still, use a special roasting tin with a dimpled lid – a little water is poured into the base of the tin at the beginning of cooking, and then the lid is removed towards the end, to allow the meat to brown. Roasting like this gives very succulent and tender results – perfect every time.

● Once the roasting time is completed, it can be difficult to judge if the meat is actually cooked – the outside may look perfect and deliciously browned, but the inside might still be a bit undercooked. The most accurate test for doneness is by checking the internal temperature with a meat thermometer. Some thermometers are inserted into the meat at the beginning of cooking and left until the end, while others are pushed into the joint about 10 minutes before the end of the calculated cooking time, to take an 'instant reading'. Always make sure that the point of the thermometer goes into a thick part of the meat, not into fat or next to bone.

Grilling

When meat is cooked on the rack under a grill, any fat will drip away from the meat and into the pan below, which makes grilling one of the healthiest methods of cooking. The only drawback is that very lean meat can dry out during grilling.

● Brush a little oil over all surfaces of the meat before cooking, or baste it during cooking with a mixture containing oil. You can also add moisture by marinating the meat beforehand, depending on how much time you have.

● Take care with the heat source and the distance the meat is

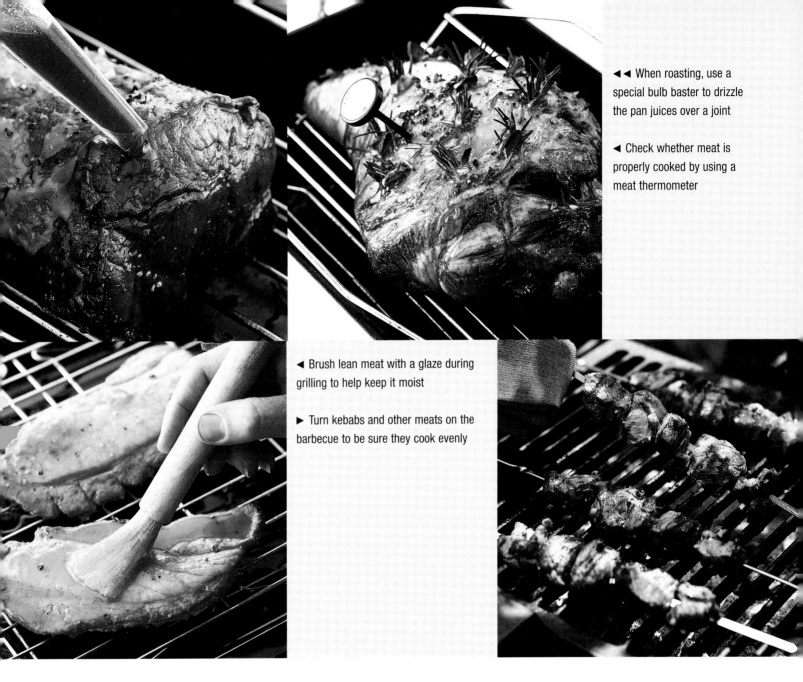

◄◄ When roasting, use a special bulb baster to drizzle the pan juices over a joint

◄ Check whether meat is properly cooked by using a meat thermometer

◄ Brush lean meat with a glaze during grilling to help keep it moist

► Turn kebabs and other meats on the barbecue to be sure they cook evenly

from it. If the heat is too fierce and the meat too close to it, the outside of the meat will be browned before the inside is properly cooked. To gauge timing accurately, preheat the grill.

Barbecuing

Anything that can be grilled can also be barbecued, so when the weather is fine, use the barbecue to cook steaks, chops, cutlets, sausages, home-made burgers and kebabs, as well as larger pieces of meat such as a butterflied whole leg of lamb.
• To help keep lean meat moist and give it a good flavour, marinate it before cooking, and baste it with a little oil or a flavourful mixture while it is on the barbecue grid. Use a special long-handled brush for basting, as the fire is very hot and oil and fat dropping onto the hot coals will spit.
• The heat of the fire is important for successful cooking. If the coals are too hot the meat may char on the outside and yet

The most nutritious results

When meat is cooked, by whatever method, it loses juices. Soluble vitamins, such as from the B group, and some minerals are carried off in the juices, as is some of the fat-soluble vitamin A. Using the juices in a gravy or sauce will retain most of these valuable nutrients.

still be raw in the centre. To safeguard against this, wait until all the flames have died down and the coals have turned from red to grey before putting the meat on to cook.

• Always make sure the meat is thoroughly cooked and piping hot before serving. If you are in any doubt with thick cuts of meat, you can always use a meat thermometer to check the internal temperature.

Griddling

This is a confusing term because it's actually a method of frying. A special ridged cast-iron grill pan is used over a high heat on top of the cooker – the pan's ridges give the meat charred stripes on the surface, which is why it is sometimes referred to as 'char-grilling', especially by chefs. Griddling is an excellent healthy way to cook steaks, chops, escalopes and other lean cuts because very little oil is needed and the meat is cooked very quickly. Also, the stripes on the meat make it look attractive and taste delicious.

• Use a pan with a thick base – the heavier the better.

• Heat the pan thoroughly before you put in the meat, usually for 10 minutes.

• Griddling causes a lot of smoke, so be sure to turn the extractor fan on high.

Frying

There are other healthy methods of frying besides griddling.

• Dry-frying, which uses no fat at all, is the healthiest option for more fatty meat such as mince, sausages and bacon – their natural fat melts out and prevents the meat from sticking to the pan. All you need is a good non-stick frying pan. After cooking, drain mince in a sieve; take sausages and bacon from the pan with a draining spoon and drain well on kitchen paper.

• Shallow-frying, or pan-frying, is excellent for thin cuts of

meat. Use a heavy non-stick pan and heat it before adding just a little oil to prevent sticking. The oil can be applied in a drizzle or rubbed on with a wad of kitchen paper. Even better, spray on the oil from a special mister, which gives a very light and even coating to the pan. Be sure the oil is hot before you put in the meat so that it browns quickly and doesn't absorb the oil. Then you can reduce the heat to finish the cooking, if necessary.

• Stir-frying in a wok uses the minimum amount of oil, and the meat is cut into thin strips so that it cooks very quickly. It's an excellent way to combine a small amount of meat with rice or noodles and lots of vegetables, to make a quick meal in one pan. Groundnut oil is good for stir-frying because it can be heated to a high temperature without burning, but you can also use sunflower, corn or olive oil. For extra flavour, add a little walnut or sesame oil too. If you haven't got a wok, you can use a deep frying pan or sauté pan instead.

Stewing, braising, casseroling and pot roasting

These are slow, moist methods of cooking at low temperatures, either in the oven or on top of the cooker. They help to tenderise the less expensive, more coarse-grained cuts of meat like beef brisket, pork shoulder and lamb chump chops. Braising traditionally uses slices of meat, while stews and casseroles use cubes. Whole large pieces or joints and pieces of meat on the bone make succulent pot roasts.

• Use a well-flavoured stock and/or wine, cider or beer, plus lots of herbs and spices, to get the best flavour. Add lots of vegetables to provide extra interest and nutritional value.

• Starchy carbohydrates such as rice, pasta and dumplings can be added near the end of cooking, to add nutritious bulk and help 'stretch' meat. Or you can turn a casserole or stew into a satisfying meal-in-a-pot by topping it with a thick layer of sliced potatoes about an hour before cooking time finishes. Cook uncovered so the potatoes turn crisp and golden brown.

Microwaving

Using a microwave speeds up meat cookery and can be very successful, especially if your oven has a browning element or browning dish to give the meat an attractive appearance. Follow the manufacturer's instructions for cooking times as these vary according to the model and power of each machine.

▲ Make a nutritious gravy from the cooking juices of roast meat

◄ Dry-fry minced meat at the beginning of cooking so the fat will melt out. It can then be strained off and discarded

▼ Stir-frying in a wok is quick and very healthy as it uses a very small amount of oil

▲ A cast-iron grill pan gives meat an attractive 'griddled' look, and it needs hardly any fat

► To use the minimum amount of oil, spray it from a special mister

▼ Long, slow casserole cooking with vegetables and flavourings makes cheaper cuts of meat very tender

Safe handling

Raw meat can contain bacteria that cause food poisoning, so it needs to be stored and prepared with care. A few simple precautions and some good kitchen sense will ensure that meat is as safe as it is good for you.

Effective hygiene
These precautions will safeguard against any bacteria transferring from raw meat to other foods:
- Thoroughly wash hands, equipment and surfaces before and after handling raw meat.
- Use separate chopping boards and knives for cutting raw meat and any food that will not be cooked before eating.

Storing meat in the fridge
For storage, keep raw meat in its original wrapping, transfer it to a covered dish or wrap it in fresh cling film or foil. Be sure to store raw and cooked meats separately, and place raw meat on a lower shelf than cooked food or food that will not be cooked before eating. This will avoid contamination from blood that might drip from the raw meat. Check regularly that your fridge is running no higher than 5°C (41°F).

Storing meat in the freezer
Before shopping, it's a good idea to turn the switch to 'super-freeze' or 'fast-freeze' if you know that you will be freezing a lot of items on your return. If the freezer is very cold – lower than the standard temperature of -18°C – meat will freeze more quickly. This helps to prevent ice crystals from forming, which would otherwise spoil the texture of the meat. Wrap steaks, chops and similar items individually in cling film or foil for easy separation later. Be sure to label each packet clearly with contents and date – once frozen it can be hard to tell what's inside the wrapping.

If you are buying meat that is already frozen, make it your last purchase and hurry home to place it in the freezer quickly before it starts to thaw. Taking a cool box with you is a great help, especially in hot weather.

Storage times for raw meat

	Fridge	Freezer
beef	3 days	9–12 months
lamb	3 days	6–9 months
pork	2 days	4–6 months
bacon rashers	3 days	1 month
vacuum-packed bacon rashers (unopened)	1–2 weeks	3 months
bacon joints	3 days	3 months
minced meat and offal	1 day	3 months
sausages	3 days	3 months

Note: The freezer storage times are a guide to the times beyond which the flavour and texture of meat may deteriorate, even though it is still safe to eat. It is preferable to have a quick turnover.

Thawing meat
Meat is best thawed in its wrappings in the fridge, but for speed you can use a microwave oven – check manufacturer's instructions. Meat must be completely thawed before cooking, and once thawed, it should be cooked as soon as possible. Never re-freeze raw meat. However, after cooking, it can be re-frozen. For example, you can thaw frozen braising steak, cook it in a casserole and then freeze the casserole.

Enjoying the leftovers
Any leftovers of cooked meat or a cooked meat dish should be cooled quickly (no longer than 2 hours at room temperature), then covered and placed in the fridge. Once cold they can be frozen. A cooked meat dish should only be reheated once. Make sure it is piping hot in the centre. Frozen cooked meat dishes must be completely thawed before thorough reheating.

Meat stock

A home-made stock beats cubes, powders and pastes from the flavour point of view and it is also salt-free, which many of the chilled stocks sold in supermarkets are not. When you use the stock in a recipe you can add salt to taste, depending on the other ingredients.

Beef, veal or lamb stock

Makes about 1.2 litres (2 pints)
900 g (2 lb) meat bones (beef, veal or lamb), chopped
2 sprigs of fresh thyme
2 sprigs of parsley
1 large bay leaf
7.5 cm (3 in) piece celery
2 onions, roughly chopped
2 celery sticks, roughly chopped
2 carrots, roughly chopped
4 peppercorns

Preparation time: 20 minutes, plus chilling
Cooking time: 5–6 hours

1 Place the bones in a large saucepan and add about 2 litres (3½ pints) water, enough to cover the bones. Bring to the boil, skimming off the scum as it rises to the surface.
2 Tie the thyme, parsley, bay leaf and celery into a bouquet garni and add to the pan with the onions, celery, carrots and peppercorns. Cover and simmer gently for 5–6 hours.
3 Strain the stock through a sieve into a bowl, discarding the bones and vegetables. Leave to cool, then chill until the fat has risen to the surface of the stock and solidified. Lift the fat off the surface and discard before using the stock.

Some more ideas
• If you prefer a richer, brown stock, first roast the bones in a 230ºC (450ºF, gas mark 8) oven for 40 minutes.
• For a non-bone stock, brown a 125 g (4½ oz) piece of stewing beef or lean boneless lamb or pork in 1 tbsp sunflower oil in a large saucepan. Remove the meat, and add 1 onion,

1 carrot and 1 celery stick, all roughly chopped, to the pan. Brown the vegetables, then pour in 2 litres (3½ pints) water and bring to the boil. Replace the meat and heat until simmering again, skimming as necessary, then add 2 bay leaves, 1 sprig each of parsley and fresh thyme, 10 black peppercorns and ½ tsp salt. Reduce the heat, cover and simmer for 2 hours. Strain, cool and remove the fat as above. This will make about 1.2 litres (2 pints).
• After chilling the stock and removing the fat, you can boil it until reduced and concentrated in flavour, then cool and freeze it in ice-cube trays to make frozen 'stock cubes'. These can then be packed together in a freezer bag and used individually – simply add them frozen to hot liquids in soups, casseroles and stews. They will melt almost instantly.

mighty meat

Meat in Minutes

Quick-and-easy meals in 30 minutes

Lean, top-quality meat doesn't take much preparation or
cooking, so it's the ideal choice when you're in a hurry
and want a healthy meal really fast. Grilled steaks and
chops are a favourite choice, served with salad in a
sandwich, or with a grain like couscous or rice, or with a
simple sauce. Oriental stir-fries are the ultimate fast food
and strips of tender meat go a long way when tossed in
the wok with noodles and crunchy vegetables. Try beef
the Japanese way with quick-cooking soba noodles, or
pork Chinese-style with five-spice
and lots of colourful vegetables.
And for the children, gammon
with pineapple and a sweet mango
glaze will always be a winner.

Steak sandwich

This bumper sandwich is made with half-size ciabatta loaves baked until warm and crusty, then split and packed with quick-fried, thinly sliced steak and salad for a healthy and filling meal. If you just need a fast supper for one, scale the recipe down and use one half-size ciabatta loaf and 85 g (3 oz) steak.

Serves 4

4 ready-to-bake half ciabatta loaves, about
  150 g (5½ oz) each
12 thin slices flash-fry or sandwich steak,
  about 340 g (12 oz) in total
2 tsp extra virgin olive oil
3 tbsp black olive paste (tapenade)
4 tomatoes, about 340 g (12 oz) in total,
  sliced
45 g (1½ oz) rocket leaves
juice of ½ lemon
salt and pepper

Preparation and cooking time: about 20 minutes

1 Preheat the oven to 200°C (400°F, gas mark 6). Bake the ciabatta for 8–10 minutes or according to the packet instructions. Remove the bread from the oven and keep warm.

2 Heat a ridged cast-iron grill pan or non-stick frying pan until hot. Season the steak with salt and pepper to taste. Brush the pan with the oil, then add the steak slices, in batches if necessary, and cook for 30 seconds on each side for rare, 1 minute on each side for medium to well-done.

3 Quickly split each loaf in half lengthways. Spread the bottom halves with the olive paste. Cover with sliced tomatoes and top with the steak.

4 Toss the rocket leaves with the lemon juice. Pile on top of the steak, then drizzle the pan juices over and top with the remaining bread halves. Serve immediately, with more rocket and sliced tomatoes.

mayonnaise and spread over the bottom halves. Top with 55 g (2 oz) mixed salad leaves or watercress tossed with lemon juice and salt and pepper to taste, then add the steak. Drizzle with the pan juices and top with the remaining toasted bread halves.

- Sliced and toasted focaccia, walnut bread or multigrain bread also make delicious sandwiches, as does toasted pitta bread or warmed flat Arab bread or flour tortillas (which are ideal to wrap around a filling).
- Well-trimmed lean sirloin steaks can be used instead of thin steak slices. The steaks can be left whole or sliced diagonally.
- Add extra flavour by frying the steak in a herb-flavoured oil or by mixing herbs with the rocket. Try torn fresh basil leaves or chopped fresh marjoram.

Each serving provides

kcal 500, **protein** 31 g, **fat** 13 g (of which saturated fat 4 g), **carbohydrate** 66 g (of which sugars 4 g), **fibre** 4 g

✓✓✓	B_1, B_6, B_{12}, E, niacin
✓✓	C, iron, zinc
✓	A, B_2, folate

Some more ideas

- For a slightly different toasted sandwich, fry 2 thinly sliced red onions in 1 tbsp extra virgin olive oil for 5 minutes or until softened and just browned. Lift out of the pan with a draining spoon and set aside. Fry the steak. Split and toast 4 baguettines (short French sticks). Mix 2 tsp sun-dried tomato paste with 2 tbsp

Plus points

- Olives have a relatively high fat content compared with other fruit and vegetables, but most of it is the unsaturated type, which is believed to be the healthiest kind of fat to consume.
- Beef is now far leaner than it used to be, and well-trimmed lean cuts such as rump steak can contain as little as 4.1% fat.

Aromatic spiced lamb cutlets

The ingredients in this delicious Middle Eastern main dish offer a good range of nutrients, including lots of vitamins and minerals. In addition, the dish is very quick and easy to make.

Serves 4

8 lamb best end of neck cutlets, about
   400 g (14 oz) in total, trimmed of fat

1 tsp cumin seeds

1 tsp coriander seeds

juice of ½ lemon

2 garlic cloves, crushed

2 tbsp extra virgin olive oil

salt and pepper

sprigs of fresh mint to garnish

Minted yogurt sauce

¼ cucumber

150 g (5½ oz) plain low-fat yogurt

1 garlic clove, crushed

1 tsp bottled mint sauce

1 tbsp chopped fresh mint

Apricot and almond couscous

280 g (10 oz) couscous

100 g (3½ oz) dried apricots, chopped

500 ml (17 fl oz) boiling vegetable stock

50 g (1¾ oz) whole blanched almonds,
   toasted

2 tbsp chopped fresh mint

2 tbsp chopped fresh coriander

juice of ½ lemon

2 tbsp extra virgin olive oil

Preparation time: 15 minutes
Cooking time: 12–14 minutes

1 Preheat the grill to high. Place the lamb cutlets in a shallow dish. Grind the cumin and coriander seeds briefly in a pestle and mortar to crack them, then mix with the lemon juice, garlic and oil, and season with salt and pepper to taste. Pour the mixture over the lamb cutlets, turn them over to coat both sides and set aside to marinate while you make the sauce.

2 Cut the cucumber in half lengthways and scoop out the seeds with a teaspoon. Grate the cucumber coarsely and drain off any excess water. Mix with the yogurt, garlic, mint sauce and fresh mint. Set aside.

3 Place the lamb cutlets on the rack in the grill pan and grill for 10–12 minutes, turning once. The cutlets will be medium-rare; if you prefer them medium to well-done cook for 12–14 minutes.

4 Meanwhile, put the couscous and apricots in a large bowl and pour over the boiling stock. Stir well, then cover with a plate and set aside to soak for 5 minutes.

5 Stir the almonds, chopped mint and coriander, lemon juice and oil into the couscous. Spoon the couscous onto plates, top each serving with 2 lamb cutlets and put a spoonful of the sauce on the side. Garnish with sprigs of fresh mint and serve immediately.

Plus points

- Almonds are a source of fibre, vitamin E and several minerals. They are also high in fat, although most of it is unsaturated.

- People in Hunza, a region in northern Kashmir, are famous for their long lives – and some have put this down to eating dried apricots. Whether true or not, dried apricots are a good source of fibre and iron and a useful source of vitamin A.

- Couscous is low in fat and high in starchy carbohydrate. It scores low on the Glycaemic Index scale, which means that it breaks down slowly in the body, releasing energy gradually into the bloodstream.

- There are over 30 varieties of mint, all containing oils that have antiseptic properties. Mint is also believed to relieve indigestion – peppermint tea made from fresh mint leaves is drunk throughout the Middle East as an aid to digestion.

Each serving provides

kcal 615, **protein** 39 g, **fat** 30 g (of which saturated fat 8 g), **carbohydrate** 51 g (of which sugars 15 g), **fibre** 3 g

✓✓✓	B_1, B_6, B_{12}, E, niacin, iron, zinc
✓✓	B_2
✓	C, folate, selenium

meat in minutes

Another idea

• Trim the fat from 400 g (14 oz) lean lamb neck fillet, cut the meat across the grain into strips and toss in the marinade. Heat a ridged cast-iron grill pan or non-stick frying pan over a moderate heat until hot. Brush with a little olive oil, then cook the lamb strips in batches for 2–3 minutes or until tender, turning them often. Finely shred 170 g (6 oz) cos lettuce and mix with 1 thinly sliced red onion, 1 coarsely grated carrot and the juice of ½ lemon. Spoon into warmed pitta breads and add the lamb strips. Top with some of the yogurt and cucumber sauce, add a drizzle of hot chilli sauce if you like, and serve immediately.

Japanese beef with soba noodles

Here strips of tender steak are coated in an intensely flavoured mixture, then stir-fried and tossed with vegetables and buckwheat noodles to make an all-in-one supper dish. The Japanese ingredients – nori, wasabi, soba and dashi powder – are available from large supermarkets, health food shops and Oriental food stores.

Serves 4

5 tbsp dark soy sauce

2 garlic cloves, crushed

1 tbsp cornflour

1 tsp wasabi paste (Japanese horseradish)

450 g (1 lb) lean sirloin steak, trimmed of fat and cut into strips

300 g (10½ oz) soba (Japanese buckwheat noodles)

2 tbsp sunflower oil

1 large red pepper, seeded and thinly sliced

1 bunch of spring onions, sliced diagonally into 5 cm (2 in) lengths

125 g (4½ oz) shiitake mushrooms, sliced

750 ml (1¼ pints) dashi stock, made with dashi powder

1 sheet nori (Japanese seaweed), cut into thin strips

15 g (½ oz) fresh coriander, chopped

Preparation and cooking time: 30 minutes

Each serving provides

kcal 534, **protein** 36 g, **fat** 11 g (of which saturated fat 3 g), **carbohydrate** 70 g (of which sugars 4 g), **fibre** 5 g

✓✓✓	B_1, B_2, B_6, B_{12}, C, E, niacin, zinc
✓✓	folate, copper, potassium
✓	iron, magnesium, selenium

1 Mix together 3 tbsp of the soy sauce, the garlic, cornflour and wasabi in a medium-sized bowl. Add the beef and stir until well coated. Set aside.

2 Bring a saucepan of water to the boil, add the noodles and cook for 5 minutes or according to the packet instructions.

3 Meanwhile, heat a wok or heavy-based frying pan until really hot, then add half of the oil and swirl to coat the wok. Toss in the red pepper, spring onions and mushrooms and stir-fry for 4 minutes or until softened. Remove from the wok with a draining spoon. Drain the noodles well and set aside.

4 Heat the remaining oil in the wok, then add the beef and stir-fry for about 4 minutes or until just tender. Remove with the draining spoon.

5 Pour the stock and remaining 2 tbsp soy sauce into the wok and add the noodles and vegetables with the nori and coriander. Toss well, then add the beef and toss again. Pile the noodles, vegetables and beef into bowls and spoon over the broth. Serve immediately.

Some more ideas

● Beef stock, preferably home-made (see page 27), can be used instead of dashi stock.

● For a teriyaki pan-fry, omit the wasabi and replace with 1 tsp finely grated fresh root ginger and 1 tbsp dry sherry.

● For a spicier flavour, stir-fry 1 seeded and finely chopped fresh red chilli with the vegetables.

● In place of the mushrooms, use 100 g (3½ oz) each baby leaf spinach and bean sprouts, adding them at the end of cooking.

Plus points

● Nori is a good source of iodine, essential for the healthy function of the thyroid gland. It is also a good source of vitamin B_{12}, being one of the few plant sources of this vitamin.

● Garlic and spring onions can help to prevent high blood pressure and high cholesterol levels, which in turn helps to prevent coronary heart disease, heart attacks and strokes. These pungent ingredients also contain allicin, a phytochemical with anti-fungal and antibiotic properties.

Glazed gammon and pineapple

Broaden your children's tea repertoire with this healthy version of a long-time favourite. Gammon steaks are quickly grilled, then topped with naturally sweet pineapple and glazed with mild mango chutney. Rice and mixed vegetables complete the meal, and a yummy orange sauce is drizzled over all.

Serves 4

250 g (8½ oz) long-grain rice

2 smoked gammon steaks, about 225 g (8 oz) each, trimmed of fat

1 can pineapple rings in natural juice, about 227 g

2 tbsp mango chutney

300 ml (10 fl oz) orange juice

100 g (3½ oz) frozen peas

100 g (3½ oz) frozen sweetcorn

1 tbsp cornflour

pepper

Preparation and cooking time: 30 minutes

Each serving provides

kcal 502, **protein** 27 g, **fat** 10 g (of which saturated fat 3 g), **carbohydrate** 81 g (of which sugars 18 g), **fibre** 3 g

✓✓✓	B₁, B₆, B₁₂, C, niacin
✓✓	B₁₂, folate, selenium, zinc
✓	iron

1 Cook the rice in a saucepan of boiling water for 10–12 minutes, or according to the packet instructions, until tender.

2 Meanwhile, preheat the grill to high. Halve the gammon steaks and snip through the curved edges at intervals so the steaks will not curl during cooking. Put the steaks in the bottom of the grill pan and cook 5 cm (2 in) away from the heat for 5 minutes.

3 Turn the steaks over. Drain the pineapple, reserving the juice, and cut each ring in half. Arrange 2 halves on each steak and sprinkle with a little pepper. Spread the mango chutney over the steaks and pineapple. Mix the pineapple juice from the can with the orange juice and pour around the steaks. Grill for 5 more minutes or until the gammon is cooked through.

4 When the rice is tender, stir in the frozen vegetables. Cook for 2 minutes or until hot, then drain off any excess water. Spoon the rice onto plates, then place the gammon steaks and pineapple alongside.

5 Pour the juices from the grill pan into a small saucepan, stir in the cornflour and bring to the boil. Cook, stirring, for 1–2 minutes or until thickened. Season with pepper, then drizzle over the rice and gammon.

Some more ideas

● For a spicier topping, sprinkle some chopped fresh chilli or crushed dried chillies over the pineapple.

● A delicious alternative to pineapple and mango is 1 small thinly sliced red onion, 1 diced Gala apple and 2 tbsp cranberry sauce. Make the sauce with 200 ml (7 fl oz) each apple and orange juice.

● Top the gammon steaks with a cheat's Cumberland sauce: mix together the grated zest of 1 lemon and 1 orange, 2 tbsp redcurrant jelly, 2 tsp wholegrain mustard, 120 ml (4 fl oz) red wine and 200 ml (7 fl oz) orange juice.

● Instead of rice, cook 225 g (8 oz) bulghur wheat in 1.2 litres (2 pints) boiling chicken or vegetable stock for 10 minutes, then mix in the frozen vegetables.

Plus points

● 100% of the adult RNI for vitamin C is provided by the orange juice, pineapple and peas in each serving.

● Frozen vegetables often contain more vitamin C than fresh vegetables. For example, frozen peas retain 60–70% of their vitamin C content after freezing and maintain this level throughout storage.

Hot harissa lamb in pitta pouches

Warm pitta bread stuffed with spicy lamb and crisp salad makes a quick and tasty light lunch. In this North African-style recipe, lean lamb is stir-fried with garlic, ginger, harissa and mint for an exciting authentic flavour.

Serves 4

4 wholemeal pitta breads

2 tbsp extra virgin olive oil

400 g (14 oz) boneless leg of lamb or neck fillet, trimmed of fat and thinly sliced

1 large garlic clove, crushed

1 tbsp finely chopped fresh root ginger

2 tsp harissa (hot chilli sauce)

4 tbsp roughly chopped fresh mint or coriander, or to taste

4 tbsp plain low-fat yogurt

Cucumber salad

100 g (3½ oz) crisp green salad leaves, shredded

½ red onion, thinly sliced

7.5 cm (3 in) piece cucumber, diced

juice of ½ lemon

salt and pepper

Preparation and cooking time: 25–30 minutes

1 First prepare the salad and pitta. Combine the salad leaves, red onion and cucumber in a bowl. Sprinkle over the lemon juice, season with salt and pepper to taste and toss together. Using a sharp knife, split the pitta breads open down one side to make pouches. Set the salad and pitta aside.

2 Preheat the grill to high. Heat a wok or heavy-based frying pan until really hot, then add the oil and swirl to coat the wok. Add the lamb, garlic and ginger, and stir-fry for 4–5 minutes or until lightly browned. Add the harissa and stir-fry for a further 2 minutes. Reduce the heat to very low and keep the lamb warm.

3 Place the pitta on the rack of the grill pan and grill for 1 minute on each side or until warm. Meanwhile, increase the heat under the lamb, add the mint or coriander and toss together.

4 Divide the lamb and salad among the warmed pitta pouches, top each serving with 1 tbsp yogurt and serve immediately.

Some more ideas

● If you can't get North African harissa, use another chilli sauce, or a few drops of Tabasco sauce. Or, if you think these may be too spicy, use 2 tsp sun-dried tomato paste instead.

● Chickpeas are a great addition to these pouches. Use only 250 g (8½ oz) lamb and add a can of chickpeas, about 400 g, drained and rinsed, with the harissa in step 2. Alternatively, for a vegetarian version, omit the lamb altogether and stir-fry the garlic and ginger with the chickpeas, then add the harissa and mint. Spread the insides of the pittas with hummus before putting in the filling.

● In place of pitta bread, wrap the lamb and salad in warmed flour tortillas or Californian flat bread. To warm these, wrap them, stacked together, in foil and heat in a 180ºC (350ºF, gas mark 4) oven for 4–5 minutes, or according to the packet instructions.

Plus points

● Each 100 g (3½ oz) serving of lamb provides over 50% of the adult RNI for zinc, a mineral that is vital for normal growth, reproduction and immunity. Zinc is also involved in the release of insulin from the pancreas, which controls blood sugar levels.

● Weight for weight, wholemeal pitta bread contains more than twice as much fibre as white pitta, and also provides higher levels of B vitamins.

● Sprinkling the salad with lemon juice not only adds a fresh, zingy flavour but also boosts the vitamin C content of this dish. With the natural fat in the lamb, there is no need to use an oily dressing.

Each serving provides

kcal 480, protein 28 g, fat 21 g (of which saturated fat 7 g), carbohydrate 48 g (of which sugars 6 g), fibre 5 g

✓✓✓	B₁, B₆, B₁₂, E, niacin, zinc
✓✓	C, folate, iron
✓	B₂, calcium, potassium

meat in minutes

38

Five-spice pork

The simple Oriental technique of stir-frying is perfect for preparing meals in a hurry. It is also a great healthy cooking method because it uses just a small amount of oil and cooks vegetables quickly so that most of their beneficial vitamins and minerals are preserved.

Serves 4

400 g (14 oz) pork fillet (tenderloin), trimmed of fat

250 g (8½ oz) medium Chinese egg noodles

1 tbsp sunflower oil

1 large onion, finely chopped

1 large garlic clove, crushed

1 tbsp five-spice powder

300 g (10½ oz) mange-tout or sugarsnap peas

2 large red peppers (or 1 red and 1 yellow or orange), seeded and thinly sliced

120 ml (4 fl oz) hot vegetable stock

salt and pepper

fresh coriander leaves to garnish

Preparation and cooking time: 30 minutes

1 Cut the pork fillet across into 5 mm (¼ in) slices, then cut each slice into 5 mm (¼ in) strips. Cover the meat and set aside.

2 Cook the noodles in a saucepan of boiling water for 4 minutes, or cook or soak them according to the packet instructions. Drain the noodles well and set aside.

3 While the noodles are cooking, heat a wok or a large heavy-based frying pan until hot. Add the oil and swirl to coat the wok, then add the onion and garlic and stir-fry for 1 minute. Add the five-spice powder and stir-fry for another minute.

4 Add the pork strips to the wok and stir-fry for 3 minutes. Add the mange-tout or sugarsnap peas and the peppers and stir-fry for a further 2 minutes. Pour in the stock, stir well and bring to the boil.

5 Add the noodles to the wok and stir and toss for 2–3 minutes or until all the ingredients are well combined. Season to taste and serve immediately, sprinkled with coriander leaves.

Some more ideas

● To reduce the fat content of this dish even further, use just 250 g (8½ oz) pork and add 250 g (8½ oz) firm tofu. Drain the tofu well and cut it into 2.5 cm (1 in) cubes, then add in step 5 with the mange-tout and peppers. Add 2 tbsp light soy sauce with the stock.

● For a vegetarian dish, replace the pork with 450 g (1 lb) drained and diced firm tofu and add 140 g (5 oz) broccoli florets. Add the tofu and broccoli with the mange-tout and peppers in step 5, and add 75 g (2½ oz) bean sprouts with the noodles in step 6.

Plus points

● Peppers have a naturally waxy skin that helps to protect them against oxidisation and prevents loss of vitamin C during storage. As a result, their vitamin C content remains high even several weeks after harvesting.

● Heating the pan until hot before adding any oil not only helps to prevent ingredients sticking, it also means less oil is needed.

● Chinese egg noodles are a low-fat source of starchy carbohydrate as well as offering some protein. When they are eaten with ingredients high in vitamin C, such as the peppers in this recipe, the body is able to absorb the iron they contain.

Each serving provides

kcal 467, **protein** 34 g, **fat** 13 g (of which saturated fat 3 g), **carbohydrate** 58 g (of which sugars 12 g), **fibre** 6 g

✓✓✓	A, B$_1$, B$_6$, B$_{12}$, C, E, niacin, zinc
✓✓	B$_2$, folate, potassium
✓	calcium, iron, selenium

Creamy liver Stroganoff

The rich flavour of liver in a cream and wine sauce goes perfectly with earthy mushrooms – here shiitake, button and brown cap are used. Serve with rice or noodles and a green salad.

Serves 4

300 g (10½ oz) lamb's liver, trimmed

1 tbsp sunflower oil

10 g (¼ oz) butter

2 onions, chopped

75 g (2½ oz) shiitake mushrooms, sliced

150 g (5½ oz) brown cap mushrooms, quartered or sliced

200 g (7 oz) button mushrooms, quartered or sliced

3 garlic cloves, chopped

1 tbsp plain flour

360 ml (12 fl oz) dry white wine

200 ml (7 fl oz) beef or veal stock, preferably home-made (see page 27)

2 tbsp chopped fresh oregano

large pinch of freshly grated nutmeg

1 tbsp Dijon mustard

3 tbsp crème fraîche

salt and pepper

chopped fresh oregano and/or parsley to garnish (optional)

Preparation and cooking time: 30 minutes

Each serving provides

kcal 229, **protein** 19 g, **fat** 18 g (of which saturated fat 4 g), **carbohydrate** 9 g (of which sugars 5 g), **fibre** 2 g

✓✓✓ A, B₁, B₂, B₆, B₁₂, C, E, niacin, copper, iron, selenium, zinc

✓ magnesium, potassium

1 Rinse the liver and pat it dry with kitchen paper. If it is not already sliced, cut it into thin slices.

2 Heat the oil in a non-stick frying pan. Place the liver in the pan and brown quickly over a very high heat for 2 minutes, turning the slices once. The liver will not be cooked through at this point. Remove from the pan and set aside.

3 Add the butter to the pan and reduce the heat to moderate. When the butter has melted, add the onions and cook, stirring frequently, for about 5 minutes or until they are softened.

4 Add all the mushrooms and the garlic and mix well, then cook for 5 minutes. Keep the heat high so the mushrooms brown rather than stew in their juices.

5 Sprinkle the mushrooms with the flour and cook, stirring, for 1–2 minutes, then slowly pour in the wine and stock, stirring all the time. Add the oregano and nutmeg and simmer, stirring, for 3–4 minutes or until the sauce reduces and thickens.

6 Reduce the heat to low and stir in the mustard and crème fraîche. Return the liver to the pan and cook gently for 3–4 minutes. Season to taste. Spoon the liver Stroganoff onto warmed plates, sprinkle with oregano and/or parsley and serve immediately.

Plus points

● Liver is an extremely rich source of iron and zinc, and of vitamin A and many of the B vitamins, especially B₁₂. The iron is in a form that is easily absorbed by the body.

● Mushrooms provide useful amounts of the B vitamins niacin, B₆ and folate. They are also a good source of copper, which is important for healthy bones and to help the body to absorb iron from food.

Some more ideas

● You can use calf's liver instead of lamb's liver. It is more delicate in texture than lamb's liver, so take care not to overcook it.

● Chicken livers can also be used. They are rich and robust in flavour and benefit from being blanched before frying. Place the whole livers in a saucepan with cold water to cover and bring to the boil over a high heat. Reduce the heat and cook for about 5 minutes, then remove from the heat and leave to cool in the liquid for a few minutes. Drain well, rinse and slice.

● If shiitake mushrooms are unavailable, use more button or brown cap mushrooms.

● For a liver paprikash, add 2 seeded and diced peppers (red and green) and 2 tbsp paprika with the onions, and 1 can chopped tomatoes, about 225 g, with their juice, along with the wine and stock. Before serving, stir in 2 tbsp chopped fresh flat-leaf parsley.

meat in minutes

Sizzling stir-fried kidneys

This is a deliciously different way to serve kidneys – tossed with Chinese egg noodles and a medley of tender Oriental vegetables in a garlicky black bean sauce. If you love strong flavours, it's the perfect recipe for you.

Serves 2

125 g (4½ oz) fine Chinese egg noodles

170 g (6 oz) calf's kidneys

4 tbsp black bean sauce

1 tbsp sunflower oil

1 small red onion, halved lengthways and thinly sliced into half rings

1 yellow pepper, seeded and sliced

1 small fresh red chilli, seeded and finely chopped

5 cm (2 in) piece fresh root ginger, finely chopped

2 garlic cloves, finely chopped

250 g (8½ oz) bean sprouts

300 g (10½ oz) pak choy, cut into 2 cm (¾ in) pieces

50 g (1¾ oz) red chard or rocket

2 tbsp soy sauce, or to taste

salt and pepper

2 tbsp toasted sesame seeds to garnish

Preparation and cooking time: 20–25 minutes

Each serving provides

kcal 630, **protein** 26 g, **fat** 25 g (of which saturated fat 4.5 g), **carbohydrate** 72 g (of which sugars 23 g), **fibre** 12 g

✓✓✓ A, B₁, B₂, B₆, B₁₂, C, folate, niacin, iron, selenium, zinc

✓✓ calcium, potassium

1 Cook the noodles in a saucepan of boiling water for 3 minutes, or cook or soak them according to the packet instructions. Drain well and set aside.

2 Cut the kidneys into 2.5 cm (1 in) pieces, following the lobes and discarding any fat and membranes. Dilute the black bean sauce with 2 tbsp water and set aside.

3 Heat 1 tsp of the oil in a non-stick frying pan over a moderately high heat. Put in the kidneys and stir-fry for 3 minutes or until they are evenly browned. Add 1½ tbsp of the black bean sauce mixture and stir to combine. Remove from the heat and keep hot.

4 Heat a wok or heavy-based frying pan until really hot, then add the remaining oil and swirl to coat the wok. Add the onion, pepper, chilli, ginger and garlic and stir-fry for 1 minute. Add the noodles, bean sprouts, pak choy and chard or rocket. Sprinkle over 2 tbsp water and continue stir-frying for 2 minutes. The vegetables should still be crunchy, and the greens wilted.

5 Add the remaining black bean sauce mixture, the soy sauce and the kidneys. Toss well to combine, then taste for seasoning, adding more soy sauce if liked. Serve immediately, sprinkled with the sesame seeds.

Some more ideas

● Use lamb's kidneys instead of calf's kidneys. Cut them in half crossways and remove the fat and membranes by incising a V-shaped indentation, then cut each half into about 8 pieces.

● Instead of kidneys, use 200 g (7 oz) pork fillet (tenderloin) or skinless boneless chicken breasts (fillets), cut into strips.

● Replace the pak choy with Oriental mustard greens or choy sum, or very small florets of broccoli.

● To save time, you can use 2 vacuum packs of ready-cooked Chinese noodles, about 150 g each, instead of cooking or soaking dried ones.

Plus points

● Kidneys are a very valuable source of iron and protein, and they also provide selenium, a mineral that acts as an antioxidant, protecting cells against damage by free radicals. Selenium also plays a major role in the maintenance of healthy skin and hair, and is important for fertility.

Oriental pork and cabbage rolls

Crunchy water chestnuts are combined with minced pork, soy sauce, fresh ginger and five-spice powder to make a flavoursome, Oriental-style filling for fresh green cabbage leaves. Serve with steamed white rice and a simple red pepper, chicory and onion salad for a quick-and-easy family meal.

Serves 4

500 g (1 lb 2 oz) extra-lean minced pork

1 can water chestnuts, about 220 g, drained and finely chopped

2 tsp five-spice powder

1 tbsp finely grated fresh root ginger

2 spring onions, finely chopped

2 tbsp dark soy sauce

2 garlic cloves, crushed

1 egg, beaten

8 large green cabbage leaves

450 ml (15 fl oz) hot chicken stock

2 tsp cornflour

1 tsp sweet chilli sauce, or to taste

curled strips of spring onion garnish

Preparation time: 10 minutes
Cooking time: 15 minutes

Each serving provides

kcal 234, **protein** 32 g, **fat** 7 g (of which saturated fat 2 g), **carbohydrate** 12 g (of which sugars 5 g), **fibre** 2 g

✓✓✓	B$_1$, B$_2$, B$_6$, B$_{12}$, C, niacin
✓✓	folate, selenium, zinc
✓	A, copper, iron

1 Place the pork in a bowl and add the water chestnuts, five-spice powder, ginger, spring onions, soy sauce, garlic and egg. Mix thoroughly with your hands or a fork until the ingredients are well blended, then divide into 8 equal portions.

2 Cut the tough stalk from the base of each cabbage leaf with a sharp knife. Place a portion of the pork mixture in the centre of each cabbage leaf, then wrap the leaf around the filling to enclose it.

3 Pour the stock into the bottom section of a large steamer. Arrange the cabbage rolls, join side down, in one layer in the top section. Cover and steam for 15 minutes or until the cabbage is tender and the rolls are firm when pressed. Remove the top section from the steamer and keep the cabbage rolls hot.

4 Mix the cornflour with 2 tbsp water, then stir this mixture into the stock in the bottom of the steamer. Bring to the boil and simmer, stirring constantly, until slightly thickened. Add the chilli sauce.

5 Serve the cabbage rolls with the sauce spooned over and sprinkled with curls of spring onion.

Some more ideas

• Instead of flavouring the pork filling with soy sauce, use 2 tbsp hoisin sauce.

• For Chinese pork balls with wilted greens and oyster sauce, shape the pork mixture into 16 balls. Place in the steamer over the pan of stock and steam for 12 minutes. Meanwhile, heat 1 tbsp sunflower oil in a wok and stir-fry 1 sliced bunch of spring onions with 200 g (7 oz) small broccoli florets and 200 g (7 oz) sugarsnap peas for 4 minutes. Add 4 tbsp water and 200 g (7 oz) pak choy separated into leaves, and stir-fry for a further 3 minutes or until all the vegetables are tender. Finally, add 4 tbsp oyster sauce, or to taste. Serve the vegetables topped with the pork balls.

Plus points

• Extra-lean minced pork is lower in fat than minced beef or lamb and only slightly fattier than skinless chicken breast.

• Water chestnuts provide small amounts of potassium, iron and fibre, but their big advantage is that they contain no fat and very few calories.

• Cabbage, like broccoli and cauliflower, contains flavonoids, which research has shown help to suppress cancer-causing cells. It also contains the beneficial anti-cancer antioxidants, vitamins C and E.

Pork chops in barbecue sauce

A sweet and sour barbecue sauce is the perfect partner for simply cooked pork chops. With a fruit and pine nut pilaf and a mixed leaf salad, this makes a tempting and substantial midweek supper.

Serves 4

1 tbsp sunflower oil

4 boneless pork loin chops, about
   140 g (5 oz) each, trimmed of fat

100 ml (3½ fl oz) orange juice

4 tbsp clear honey

2 tbsp soy sauce

2 tbsp dry sherry

2 tbsp red wine vinegar

2 tbsp French mustard

2 tbsp tomato purée

salt and pepper

Pine nut and raisin pilaf

250 g (8½ oz) basmati rice

1 tbsp sunflower oil

1 onion, sliced

1 garlic clove, finely chopped

50 g (1¾ oz) pine nuts

50 g (1¾ oz) raisins

600 ml (1 pint) vegetable stock

Preparation and cooking time: 30 minutes

1 Heat the oil in a frying pan and add the chops. Fry for 5 minutes or until browned on both sides, turning them over once.

2 In a small bowl, blend together the orange juice, honey, soy sauce, sherry, vinegar, mustard and tomato purée. Pour over the chops, then leave to simmer for 15 minutes or until the chops are cooked through and tender, turning them once or twice.

3 Meanwhile, make the pilaf. Put the rice in a sieve and rinse under cold running water until the water is clear. Drain well. Heat the oil in a saucepan, add the onion and garlic and cook for 5 minutes or until softened and beginning to brown. Sprinkle in the pine nuts and raisins and cook, stirring, for 2–3 minutes or until the nuts turn golden brown.

4 Add the rice and stir well to mix. Pour in the stock and bring to the boil. Reduce the heat, cover and simmer for 10 minutes or until the rice is tender and all the stock has been absorbed. Season to taste.

5 To serve, spoon the pilaf onto warmed plates and arrange the chops in barbecue sauce alongside.

Some more ideas

● For a fruity sauce, omit the honey, soy sauce, vinegar and mustard and increase the orange juice to 250 ml (8½ fl oz).

● Replace the pork chops with medallions of pork fillet (tenderloin) or skinless boneless chicken breasts (fillets). The cooking time for these will be 15–20 minutes.

● Use different nuts, such as pistachios or cashews.

Plus points

● Rice is one of the most important staple crops, the very basis of life for millions of people worldwide. Polishing the grains to produce the familiar white varieties partially removes B vitamins; however, in this recipe, the pork more than makes up for this loss as it is an excellent source of vitamin B_{12} and a good source of vitamins B_1 and B_6.

● Pine nuts are a good source of vitamin E and potassium, and they also contribute useful amounts of vitamin B_1, magnesium, zinc and iron.

Each serving provides

kcal 671, **protein** 40 g, **fat** 19 g (of which saturated fat 2 g), **carbohydrate** 85 g (of which sugars 33 g), **fibre** 1 g

✓✓✓ B_1, B_6, B_{12}, E, zinc

✓✓ B_2, C, iron, magnesium, potassium, selenium

For Maximum Vitality

Raw fruit and vegetables add crunch and colour

Eaten raw, fruit and vegetables are packed with vitamins and minerals – and meat is their perfect partner. Try fillet steak Waldorf-style with carrots, radishes, apples and walnuts, or zesty Mexican marinated pork wrapped in tortillas with a fresh avocado and tomato salsa. Give strips of succulent sirloin the full Thai treatment with chilli, lime and exotic papaya, or griddle rump steak and toss into a salade niçoise. Lamb with plums is an inspired combination, especially wrapped in rice papers and served with a sesame dipping sauce.

Beef Waldorf

Raw vegetables and fruits are one of the richest sources of essential vitamins and minerals. This tasty main-dish salad offers plenty of these vital nutrients and it's made extra delicious with a creamy mustard dressing. Serve with lots of crusty fresh bread for a satisfying and healthy meal.

Serves 4

2 fillet steaks, about 140 g (5 oz) each, trimmed of fat

¼ tsp extra virgin olive oil

250 g (8½ oz) radishes, thinly sliced

3 carrots, grated

1 small yellow pepper, seeded and cut into thin rings

3 celery sticks, sliced diagonally

3 spring onions, sliced diagonally

30 g (1 oz) walnuts

55 g (2 oz) raisins or sultanas

2 small dessert apples

2 tsp lemon juice

100 g (3½ oz) rocket or watercress

salt and pepper

Mustard dressing

2 tbsp wholegrain mustard

3 tbsp mayonnaise

3 tbsp Greek-style yogurt

Preparation time: 25–30 minutes, plus 15 minutes cooling

Each serving provides

kcal 300, **protein** 18 g, **fat** 15 g (of which saturated fat 3 g), **carbohydrate** 25 g (of which sugars 25 g), **fibre** 5 g

✓✓✓	A, B₁, B₆, B₁₂, E, niacin
✓✓	B₂, folate, iron, potassium, zinc
✓	calcium, selenium

1 Brush the steaks with the oil and season with pepper. Heat a ridged cast-iron grill pan or non-stick frying pan over a moderately high heat until hot. Put in the steaks and cook for 3 minutes on each side for medium-rare or 4 minutes on each side for medium. These cooking times are for 2 cm (¾ in) steaks; adjust slightly for more or less than this thickness. Remove the steaks from the pan and leave to cool for at least 15 minutes.

2 Meanwhile, make the dressing. Put the mustard, mayonnaise and yogurt in a small bowl and stir together until well combined.

3 Put the radishes, carrots, yellow pepper, celery, spring onions, walnuts and raisins or sultanas in a large bowl. Quarter and core the apples, then cut them into 2 cm (¾ in) chunks and toss in the lemon juice. Add to the bowl with half of the dressing and turn to coat everything well. Season with salt and pepper to taste.

4 To serve, pile the rocket or watercress on 4 plates and spoon the apple and vegetable salad alongside. Cut the steak into thin slices and arrange on top. Spoon over the remaining dressing or hand it round separately in a jug.

Some more ideas

• Instead of fillet steak, use a 280 g (10 oz) lean sirloin steak, cut about 2 cm (¾ in) thick, trimmed of fat.

• Use the large white radish called mooli or daikon instead of red radishes. It is easy to grate by hand or in a food processor.

• For a roast beef and rice Waldorf, mix 300 g (10½ oz) cubed leftover roast beef and 250 g (8½ oz) brown rice, cooked and cooled, into the apple and vegetable salad. This Waldorf salad is also good made with cooked chicken.

Plus points

• Apples provide good amounts of vitamin C as well as soluble fibre in the form of pectin. Eating apples with their skin offers the maximum amount of fibre.

• All the sugars in this dish are in the 'intrinsic' form, which means they are natural sugars found in fruit (the raisins and apples) and vegetables (the radishes, carrots, yellow pepper, celery, spring onions and watercress). Fibre in the fruit and vegetables controls the rate at which these sugars are absorbed into the blood.

for maximum vitality

Mexican pork

Lean pork marinated in a zesty Mexican spice and citrus mixture is griddled until succulent, then sliced thinly and served in soft flour tortillas. The finishing touch is a fresh avocado salsa.

Serves 4

400 g (14 oz) pork fillet (tenderloin), trimmed of fat

2 tsp extra virgin olive oil

2 onions, thickly sliced

2 peppers (1 red and 1 yellow), seeded and cut into chunks

4 large tomato-flavoured flour tortillas

Citrus marinade

3 garlic cloves, chopped

juice of 1 lime

juice of ½ grapefruit or 1 small blood orange

2 tsp mild chilli powder

1 tsp paprika

½ tsp ground cumin

¼ tsp dried oregano or mixed herbs such as herbes de Provence

pinch of ground cinnamon

3 spring onions, chopped

1 tbsp extra virgin olive oil

Avocado and radish salsa

1 avocado

3 radishes, diced

1 garlic clove, chopped

1 ripe tomato, diced

juice of ½ lime, or to taste

1 spring onion, chopped

1 tbsp chopped fresh coriander

salt and pepper

Preparation and cooking time: about 50 minutes, plus at least 30 minutes marinating

1 Mix together all the ingredients for the marinade in a shallow dish. Add the pork fillet and turn to coat. Cover and marinate for at least 30 minutes, or overnight.

2 To prepare the salsa, halve, stone and peel the avocado, then mash the flesh in a bowl. Add the remaining salsa ingredients and mix well, then season to taste. Cover and chill until serving time.

3 Preheat the oven to 180°C (350°F, gas mark 4). Heat a ridged cast-iron grill pan or non-stick frying pan over a moderate heat until hot. Remove the meat from its marinade and pat it dry with kitchen paper. Brush the pan with the olive oil, then add the pork and sear on all sides.

4 Push the pork to one side and add the onions and peppers to the pan. Cook for 12–15 minutes or until the vegetables are tender and lightly charred and the pork is cooked through.

5 Meanwhile, wrap the tortillas, stacked up, in foil and put into the oven to warm for 5–10 minutes.

6 Remove the grill pan from the heat. Lift out the pork and cut it into thin strips, then return it to the pan and mix with the onions and peppers.

7 To serve, pile the pork, onions and peppers into the tortillas, roll into cone shapes and top with salsa.

Plus points

- Avocados are high in calories, mainly from the monounsaturated fat they contain. This is the same type of fat that makes olive oil so highly recommended for the prevention of coronary heart disease. Avocados are also a useful source of vitamin E, an important antioxidant, and of vitamin B_6.

- Cooking garlic destroys some of the allicin, one of the beneficial phytochemicals it contains, so for maximum health benefits it is best eaten raw.

- There is plenty of vitamin C in this dish, from the peppers and tomatoes in particular. Vitamin C plays a major role in maintaining a healthy immune system.

Each serving provides

kcal 437, **protein** 30 g, **fat** 17 g (of which saturated fat 4 g), **carbohydrate** 46 g (of which sugars 11 g), **fibre** 6 g

✓✓✓	A, B_1, B_6, B_{12}, C, E, niacin
✓✓	folate, iron
✓	calcium, potassium, zinc

Some more ideas

- Fillet, rump or sirloin of beef can be used instead of pork.
- If you can't get tomato-flavoured flour tortillas, any kind of soft flour tortilla can be used. If you prefer, you can warm them through on top of the cooker. Spray or sprinkle each one with a few drops of water, then heat in a non-stick frying pan for 15–30 seconds on each side. As each tortilla is done, wrap loosely in a clean tea towel to keep warm.
- For a change from the avocado salsa, serve with a fruity salsa. Mix together 300 g (10½ oz) sliced seedless green grapes, 1 seeded and diced satsuma or other small citrus fruit, 1 diced (unpeeled) small crisp pear, ¼ seeded and chopped fresh red chilli, 3 chopped radishes, 1 chopped garlic clove, 1 thinly sliced spring onion, 1 tbsp each chopped fresh coriander and mint, 1 tsp sugar or honey and the juice of ½ lime or lemon. Serve chilled.

Thai beef salad with papaya

Sweet juicy papaya, crisp leaves and aromatic herbs are a sensational combination in this Thai-inspired salad. Thai fragrant rice – jasmine rice simmered in stock and scented with lime leaves – is the perfect complement.

Serves 4

2 thick-cut lean sirloin steaks, about 450 g (1 lb) in total, trimmed of fat

250 g (8½ oz) jasmine rice

1.2 litres (2 pints) chicken stock

4 fresh lime leaves, crushed

2 tsp sunflower oil

2 firm, ripe papayas, peeled, seeded and sliced

½ small cucumber, halved lengthways, seeded and sliced across

20 fresh mint leaves, shredded

15 g (½ oz) fresh coriander, chopped

1 red onion, thinly sliced

2 Little Gem lettuces, separated into leaves

Thai lime dressing

2 tbsp sunflower oil

1 tbsp clear honey

grated zest and juice of 1 lime

2 tbsp Thai fish sauce

2 tbsp light soy sauce

1 fresh red chilli, or to taste, seeded and finely chopped

2 garlic cloves, crushed

To garnish

4 tbsp roasted peanuts, roughly chopped

sprigs of fresh mint

Preparation time: 35 minutes

1 First make the dressing. Mix all the ingredients together in a small bowl. Spoon 3 tbsp over the steaks and set aside to marinate while you cook the rice. Reserve the remaining dressing.

2 Put the rice in a saucepan with the stock and lime leaves. Bring to the boil, then cover and leave to simmer for 10 minutes, or according to the packet instructions, until tender.

3 While the rice is cooking, pat the steaks dry with kitchen paper. Heat a ridged cast-iron grill pan or non-stick frying pan over a high heat until hot. Brush with the oil, then add the steaks and cook for 2½ minutes on each side. The meat will be rare. Cook longer if you prefer it medium or well-done. Remove the steaks to a chopping board and leave to rest for a few minutes.

4 Place the papayas, cucumber, mint, coriander and red onion in a bowl. Add all but 2 tbsp of the remaining dressing and toss gently to mix.

5 Drain the rice well and divide among individual plates. Arrange the lettuce leaves on the plates and top with the papaya salad. Slice the beef into strips, arrange on top of the salad and spoon over the remaining dressing. Garnish with the peanuts and mint sprigs. Serve at room temperature.

Plus points

● Beef is an excellent source of zinc and a useful source of iron. Iron from red meat is far more easily absorbed by the body than iron fom vegetable sources.

● Papaya is a useful source of vitamin A (from the beta-carotene it provides), which is needed for good vision. This tropical fruit plays a vital role in preventing blindness in many parts of the world where those foods that provide most vitamin A in the UK (full-fat milk, cheese, butter, egg yolks) are not part of the average diet. Papaya also provides good amounts of vitamin C and useful amounts of the micromineral magnesium.

Each serving provides

kcal 563, **protein** 44 g, **fat** 13 g (of which saturated fat 5 g), **carbohydrate** 67 g (of which sugars 14 g), **fibre** 3 g

✓✓✓	B_1, B_6, B_{12}, C, E, niacin, zinc
✓✓	iron
✓	A, folate, potassium, selenium

for maximum vitality

Some more ideas

- You can use the grated zest of 1 lime instead of lime leaves.
- For a Thai red curry and orange dressing, mix together 2 tbsp sunflower oil, 2 tbsp light soy sauce, 1 tbsp light soft brown sugar, 1 tsp Thai red curry paste, ½ tsp grated orange zest and 3 tbsp orange juice.
- Make a Thai lamb salad. Use lean lamb leg steaks in place of the beef, and the Thai red curry and orange dressing (see left). Before cooking the lamb, put 2 quartered and seeded red peppers on the grill pan, skin side down, and cook for 4 minutes or until blackened; cool, then skin and chop. In place of the papaya salad, toss the peppers with 400 g (14 oz) halved cherry tomatoes, 100 g (3½ oz) bean sprouts and 2 thinly sliced courgettes.

Oriental lamb and plum wraps

Packed with crisp raw vegetables and juicy fruit slices, these wraps make a refreshing alternative to rich Peking duck in a Chinese meal. They are ideal for entertaining because the lamb is equally good hot or at room temperature. Serve as a main dish, or as a starter for 8, with a bowl of thinly sliced cucumber.

Serves 4 (makes 16 wraps)

500 g (1 lb 2 oz) lean lamb neck fillets, trimmed of fat

1½ tbsp soy sauce

6 spring onions

¼ cucumber, about 150 g (5½ oz)

6 sweet red plums, about 340 g (12 oz) in total

16 large, crisp romaine or cos lettuce leaves

16 rice paper wrappers

Sesame dipping sauce

5 tsp toasted sesame oil

1 tbsp finely grated fresh root ginger

½ tbsp sesame seeds

2 tsp soy sauce

1 tsp caster sugar

Preparation and cooking time: 35 minutes

Each serving provides

kcal 360, **protein** 26 g, **fat** 22 g (of which saturated fat 9 g), **carbohydrate** 15 g (of which sugars 9 g), **fibre** 3 g

✓✓✓	B₁, B₆, B₁₂, E, niacin, zinc
✓✓	copper, magnesium
✓	A, B₂, C, folate, iron, potassium, selenium

1 First make the dipping sauce. Put all the ingredients in a screw-top jar and shake well. Set aside.

2 Cut each lamb fillet lengthways into three, then cut each piece into long, thin slices. Mix the slices in a bowl with the soy sauce and set aside.

3 Cut the spring onions lengthways in half, then shred them finely. Set a few aside for garnish and put the rest on a large platter. Cut the cucumber lengthways in half and scoop out the seeds with a teaspoon, then thinly slice the cucumber halves into half moons. Add to the platter.

4 Halve the plums and remove the stones. Cut the plums into long, thin slices. Add to the platter with the spring onions and cucumber.

5 Rinse and dry the lettuce leaves and remove the central stalks. Tear off 16 pieces large enough to fit in the centre of the rice paper wrappers. Finely shred the remaining lettuce and add to the platter of vegetables and plums.

6 Heat a large non-stick frying pan over a moderately high heat until hot. Add half of the lamb slices and stir-fry for 3–5 minutes or until the meat is cooked to your liking. Using a draining spoon, transfer the meat to a plate. Stir-fry the remaining lamb and spoon onto the plate. Keep warm.

7 Pour 1 cm (½ in) hot water into a dish large enough to hold the wrappers. Place a clean tea towel on the work surface. Working with 1 wrapper at a time, dip it in the water to soften for 20–25 seconds, then transfer to the tea towel and pat dry. Immediately put a lettuce leaf in the centre of the wrapper. Top with a spoonful of lamb, then some spring onions, cucumber, plums and shredded lettuce. Fold in both sides of the wrapper, then roll up. Repeat, to make 16 rolls altogether.

8 Shake the dipping sauce, then pour it into a small bowl. Arrange the wraps on plates and scatter over the remaining spring onions. Serve with the dipping sauce handed separately.

Plus points

● Although lamb still tends to contain more fat than other meats, changes in breeding, feeding and butchery techniques mean that lean cuts only contain about one-third of the fat that they would have 20 years ago. More of the fat is monounsaturated, which is good news for healthy hearts.

● Plums offer useful amounts of fibre and beta-carotene.

for maximum vitality

Some more ideas

- This is a good way to use up leftover roast lamb, beef or pork. Cut it into thin strips.
- Instead of the cucumber and plums, use 300 g (10½ oz) each grated carrots and courgettes.
- Other vitamin-packed raw vegetables to use with either the lamb, beef or pork versions include finely shredded peppers, bean sprouts, alfalfa, shredded mange-tout, and thinly sliced button mushrooms or enoki mushrooms.
- Sprinkle the filling with finely chopped fresh coriander, chives or parsley before rolling up the wrappers.
- Chopped, drained canned water chestnuts will add extra texture to the filling.
- Chilled mango or papaya slices can be used instead of the plums.
- Pickled ginger slices, available from Japanese food stores and some supermarkets, can replace the plums for a hot, zingy flavour.
- For an extra kick, spread a tiny dab of wasabi (Japanese horseradish) on each lettuce leaf.
- For an instant dipping sauce, you can use bottled plum sauce.
- For a spicy dipping sauce, add a good pinch of crushed dried chillies.

Risi bisi ham salad

Full of crisp crunchy vegetables, lean ham and plenty of fresh herbs, this wholesome rice salad is substantial enough to serve as a main meal on its own. It makes a refreshing and tasty dish, ideal for eating al fresco in the garden or packing for a picnic on a hot summer's day.

Serves 6

340 g (12 oz) mixed basmati and wild rice
600 ml (1 pint) boiling water
150 g (5½ oz) frozen petit pois
200 g (7 oz) piece lean cooked ham, trimmed
    of fat and cut into strips
3 celery sticks, sliced
1 red onion, thinly sliced
3 tbsp chopped parsley
2 tbsp chopped fresh mint
1 head chicory, leaves separated
100 g (3½ oz) radicchio, finely shredded
salt and pepper
Fresh orange dressing
6 tbsp orange juice
3 tbsp extra virgin olive oil
2 tsp Dijon mustard

Preparation time: 25 minutes, plus cooling

Each serving provides

kcal 327, **protein** 13 g, **fat** 8 g (of which saturated fat 1 g), **carbohydrate** 52 g (of which sugars 4 g), **fibre** 2 g

✓✓✓	B$_1$, B$_6$, B$_{12}$, E
✓✓	C, folate
✓	iron, potassium, zinc

1 Put the rice in a saucepan and pour over the boiling water. Bring back to the boil, then reduce the heat to low. Cover and simmer for about 15 minutes, or according to the packet instructions, until the rice is tender and all the water has been absorbed. Tip the rice into a large bowl and stir in the frozen petit pois, then leave to cool.

2 Add the ham, celery, onion, parsley and mint and toss well. Mix together the dressing ingredients, add to the bowl and toss until all the salad ingredients are evenly coated. Season with salt and pepper to taste.

3 Reserve a few whole chicory leaves for the garnish, then finely shred the rest. Serve the rice salad and shredded chicory and radicchio on individual plates, garnished with the reserved whole chicory leaves.

Another idea

● For a risi bisi sweetcorn salad, cook 250 g (8½ oz) brown rice in twice its volume of boiling vegetable stock for 35 minutes or until tender. Drain if necessary, then set aside. Heat 2 tsp extra virgin olive oil in a small saucepan and cook 1 seeded and finely diced red pepper over a high heat for 4 minutes or until it begins to char. Leave to cool. Cook 100 g (3½ oz) fine green beans, cut into short lengths, in boiling water for 4 minutes. Drain and refresh in cold water. Chop 6 spring onions and place in a bowl with the rice, red pepper and green beans and add a can of sweetcorn kernels, about 200 g, and a can of red kidney beans, about 400 g, both drained and rinsed. Mix together 2 tbsp balsamic vinegar, 2 tbsp extra virgin olive oil, 2 tsp wholegrain mustard, ½ tsp clear honey and salt and pepper to taste. Add this dressing to the salad together with 3 tbsp chopped parsley and toss well to mix.

Plus points

● Radicchio, a member of the chicory family, has deep red and white tightly packed leaves. The red pigment means this vegetable is high in beta-carotene and other cancer-fighting phytochemicals.

● Using orange juice as a base for the dressing rather than sharp vinegar means less oil is needed. It also increases the amount of vitamin C in the dish.

● The combination of lean ham, rice and peas provides almost half of the RNI of protein for an adult woman.

for maximum vitality

Beef salade niçoise

In this hearty, French-style salad, slices of quickly griddled rump steak top a mixture of colourful vegetables in a tangy Dijon mustard dressing. Serve with a warm baguette to mop up all the delicious juices.

Serves 4

1 thick-cut lean rump steak, about 340 g (12 oz), trimmed of fat

coarsely ground black pepper

¼ tsp dried herbes de Provence, or to taste

500 g (1 lb 2 oz) small new potatoes, scrubbed

200 g (7 oz) French beans, trimmed

200 g (7 oz) shelled broad beans, fresh or frozen

200 g (7 oz) cherry tomatoes, halved

100 g (3½ oz) mixed black and green olives, stoned

2 tbsp snipped fresh chives

3 tbsp chopped parsley

100 g (3½ oz) baby leaf spinach

3 Little Gem lettuces, separated into leaves

Mustard vinaigrette

2 tbsp extra virgin olive oil

1 tbsp red wine vinegar

2 tsp Dijon mustard

salt and pepper

Preparation time: 45–50 minutes

Each serving provides

kcal 612, **protein** 37 g, **fat** 17 g (of which saturated fat 4 g), **carbohydrate** 84 g (of which sugars 8 g), **fibre** 10 g

✓✓✓ A, B$_1$, B$_6$, B$_{12}$, C, E, niacin, iron, zinc

✓✓ B$_2$

1 Pat the steak dry with kitchen paper. Season on both sides with pepper and dried herbs. Set aside.

2 Place the potatoes in a saucepan of boiling water and cook for 10 minutes. Add the French and broad beans and cook for a further 5 minutes or until all the vegetables are just tender. Drain in a colander and rinse with cold water to cool a bit.

3 Put the potatoes and beans in a large bowl and add the tomatoes, olives, chives and parsley. Set aside.

4 Heat a ridged cast-iron grill pan or a non-stick frying pan until hot. Cook the steak for 2½ minutes on each side. It will be rare; cook longer if you prefer it medium or well-done. Remove to a plate and leave to rest for 5 minutes.

5 Meanwhile, place the dressing ingredients in a screw-top jar with 2 tbsp water and season with salt and pepper to taste. Shake to mix.

6 Cut the steak into slices about 5 mm (¼ in) thick and add to the vegetables. Pour any juices that have collected on the plate into the dressing. Pour the dressing over the meat and vegetables and toss until thoroughly combined. Arrange the spinach and lettuce leaves in a large salad bowl or on a large platter. Spoon on the steak salad and serve immediately.

Some more ideas

• Veal and chicken can also be used in this salad. Replace the steak with 300 g (10½ oz) thinly sliced veal escalopes, griddled over a moderate heat for 2–2½ minutes, or 300 g (10½ oz) diced cooked chicken (without skin).

• Instead of broad beans use 2 avocados, peeled, stoned and diced.

Plus points

• Potatoes are a classic source of starchy carbohydrate for everyday meals. The preparation method makes a big difference to the amount of dietary fibre provided: new potatoes cooked in their skins offer one-third more fibre than peeled potatoes. Cooking potatoes in their skins also preserves the nutrients found just under the skin.

• Robust broad beans go well with beef and they bring valuable dietary fibre to the dish.

• Parsley has long been appreciated as a breath freshener, particularly when eaten raw with or after a dish containing garlic. Parsley is also nutritious, being a useful source of folate, iron and vitamin C.

Lamb tabbouleh with fresh herbs

In this Middle Eastern-style salad, bulghur wheat and crisp colourful salad ingredients are tossed with a generous quantity of chopped fresh herbs and a light lemony dressing, then served with succulent pieces of lean lamb. It's the perfect dish for a relaxed meal. Serve with toasted wholemeal pitta triangles and plain yogurt.

Serves 4

400 g (14 oz) lean lamb neck fillets, trimmed
   of fat
1 tbsp extra virgin olive oil
juice of ½ lemon
1 garlic clove, crushed
fresh mint leaves to garnish

Tabbouleh

250 g (8½ oz) bulghur wheat
400 ml (14 fl oz) boiling water
12 cherry tomatoes, halved
1 yellow or orange pepper, seeded and diced
7.5 cm (3 in) piece cucumber, diced
4 spring onions, sliced
handful of fresh mint, roughly chopped
handful of parsley, roughly chopped

Lemon dressing

2 tbsp extra virgin olive oil
juice of ½ lemon
1 large garlic clove, crushed
1 tsp clear honey
salt and pepper

Preparation time: about 40 minutes, plus at
   least 1 hour marinating

1 Slit open the lamb fillets lengthways, not cutting all the way through. Open the meat out flat and place in a shallow dish. Mix together the oil, lemon juice and garlic, pour over the lamb and turn it a couple of times to coat. Cover the dish with cling film and leave to marinate in the fridge for at least 1 hour, preferably overnight.

2 For the tabbouleh, place the bulghur wheat in a bowl, pour over the boiling water and leave to soak for 20 minutes or until all the water has been absorbed.

3 Mix together the ingredients for the dressing. Add the dressing to the soaked bulghur wheat together with the tomatoes, pepper, cucumber, spring onions and herbs.

4 Preheat the grill to high. Place the lamb on the rack of the grill pan and grill for 3–4 minutes on each side or until the meat is evenly browned. It will be medium-rare; cook longer if you prefer it medium or well-done.

5 Taste the tabbouleh salad for seasoning and fluff up with a fork. Slice the lamb diagonally, pile on top of the tabbouleh and garnish with mint leaves. Serve as soon as possible.

Plus points

• Bulghur wheat is not only a useful source of fibre, but like many other cereals it also provides complex (starchy) carbohydrate and B vitamins.

• Including garlic in the diet is known to be beneficial for a healthy heart. It is also thought to help clear cold symptoms and chest infections.

Each serving provides

kcal 632, **protein** 30 g, **fat** 24 g (of which saturated fat 8 g), **carbohydrate** 76 g (of which sugars 9 g), **fibre** 3 g

✓✓✓	B_1, B_6, B_{12}, C, E, niacin, copper, zinc
✓✓	B_2, iron, potassium
✓	A, folate

Some more ideas

• Cut the lamb into cubes and marinate, then thread on skewers and grill for 8–10 minutes, turning often. Lay the kebabs across the tabbouleh for serving.

• Couscous can be used in place of bulghur wheat. It only needs to be soaked in boiling water for about 5 minutes.

• Griddle the lamb rather than grilling it. Heat a ridged cast-iron grill pan over a high heat until hot. Drain the lamb well, and griddle for 3–4 minutes on each side or until browned and cooked to your taste.

• Vary the tabbouleh ingredients by replacing the tomatoes and cucumber with 75 g (2½ oz) slivered ready-to-eat dried apricots, 55 g (2 oz)

toasted hazelnuts and 100 g (3½ oz) roughly torn watercress or baby spinach leaves. Use a red pepper instead of yellow or orange.

• For a vegetarian version, use 340 g (12 oz) Quorn pieces or firm tofu, cut into cubes or strips, in place of the lamb. Marinate, then stir-fry with the marinade for 5 minutes, and toss into the tabbouleh.

Penne salad with bresaola and black olives

Fresh basil, rocket, peppers, olives and tomatoes give a summery, Mediterranean flavour to this prepare-ahead salad. It makes a nutritious main course because it's high in starchy carbohydrates with just enough protein from the bresaola, which is Italian cured beef. To complete the theme, serve it with olive ciabatta.

Serves 4

340 g (12 oz) penne or other pasta shapes

1 red pepper, halved lengthways and seeded

100 g (3½ oz) sliced bresaola, cut into thin strips

1 can stoned black olives in brine, about 185 g, drained, rinsed and sliced

4 sun-dried tomatoes in oil, patted dry and sliced

200 g (7 oz) yellow or red cherry tomatoes, cut in half

40 g (1½ oz) rocket or young spinach leaves

20 g (¾ oz) fresh basil leaves, shredded

Balsamic dressing

3 tbsp extra virgin olive oil

1 tbsp balsamic vinegar

salt and pepper

Preparation time: 30–35 minutes

Each serving provides

kcal 471, **protein** 18 g, **fat** 16 g (of which saturated fat 2 g), **carbohydrate** 68 g (of which sugars 5 g), **fibre** 4 g

✓✓✓	A, B₁, B₆, C, E, niacin
✓✓	copper, iron, magnesium
✓	B₂, folate, calcium, selenium, zinc

1 Drop the pasta into a large saucepan of boiling water. When the water returns to the boil, cook for 10–12 minutes, or according to the packet instructions, until al dente. Drain well and place in a large bowl.

2 Whisk together the oil and vinegar for the dressing, season with salt and pepper to taste and pour over the pasta. Toss well to mix, then cover and set aside.

3 Preheat the grill to high. Put the pepper halves, cut sides down, on the grill rack and grill for 5–6 minutes or until the skin is blistered and blackened all over. Place the peppers in a polythene bag and leave until they are cool enough to handle. Using your fingers and the tip of a knife, remove the skins. Cut the flesh into thin strips.

4 Add the pepper strips, bresaola, olives and sun-dried tomatoes to the pasta and mix gently together. Add the tomatoes, rocket or spinach and basil to the pasta mixture and toss the ingredients together gently with your hands, taking care not to break up the tomatoes. Taste for seasoning, and add salt and pepper if needed. Serve at room temperature.

Plus points

- Being a starchy carbohydrate, pasta is an excellent energy-giving and satisfying food for all the family. The energy is slowly released as the pasta is digested, so helping to prevent between-meal hunger pangs.
- Tomatoes and red peppers are both excellent sources of beta-carotene (the plant form of vitamin A) and vitamin C .
- Cutting, chopping or slicing tomatoes just before serving preserves as much of their vitamin C content as possible.

Some more ideas

- The salad can be prepared up to 8 hours ahead and chilled. Remove it from the fridge 15 minutes before serving to allow it to come to room temperature, and add the tomatoes, rocket and basil at the last minute.

- Instead of bresaola, you can use Parma ham.
- For a German-style potato and frankfurter salad, cook 400 g (14 oz) scrubbed new potatoes in boiling water, then drain and cool. Heat 2 frankfurters in simmering water for 3 minutes; drain and slice. Make the dressing

with 3 tbsp extra virgin olive oil, 1 tbsp white wine vinegar and 1 tsp German mustard. Cut the potatoes in half and toss with the dressing and frankfurters. Cover and chill until about 15 minutes before serving, then add 100 g (3½ oz) young spinach leaves and toss gently.

Family Favourites

Healthy dishes the whole family will enjoy

Meat makes delicious everyday meals for a growing family. It's nutritious, tasty and satisfying when there are hungry mouths to feed. For a midweek meal, what could be better than juicy bangers with lots of luscious mash, or shepherd's pie with a potato and parsnip top. Or what about toad-in-the-hole? This is good comfort food that everyone loves. You could also try long-simmered American pork and beans, or a meatloaf with a spiral of spinach. For an exotic note there's Chinese beef in oyster sauce, or Indian keema curry based on lean minced beef. And children will love the beefburgers and chilli con carne, both given a new modern twist.

Tagliatelle with meatballs

This is a variation of the ever-popular spaghetti bolognese and is sure to become just as well-loved. The little meatballs have aubergine added for a modern twist, and the sauce contains all the essential flavours of a classic Italian dish. Both can be made ahead, then simply reheated when you are ready to cook the pasta.

Serves 6

1 aubergine, about 200 g (7 oz)

2 tsp extra virgin olive oil

340 g (12 oz) lean minced beef

1 small onion, roughly chopped

1 garlic clove, crushed

100 g (3½ oz) fresh white breadcrumbs

grated zest of 1 lemon

1 tbsp fresh basil leaves

400 g (14 oz) tagliatelle made with egg

salt and pepper

fresh basil leaves to garnish

Rich tomato sauce

1 tbsp extra virgin olive oil

4 lean back bacon rashers, about
    125 g (4½ oz) in total, rinded and chopped

1 onion, roughly chopped

1 medium-sized carrot, thinly sliced

1 celery stick, thinly sliced

1 garlic clove, crushed

2 cans chopped tomatoes, about 400 g each

150 ml (5 fl oz) dry white wine

1 tbsp chopped fresh basil

Preparation and cooking time: 1¼ hours

1 Preheat the grill to high. Halve the aubergine lengthways, then place skin side up on the rack in the grill pan and grill for 5 minutes. Turn the aubergine halves over, brush each cut side with 1 tsp oil, and grill for a further 5 minutes or until the flesh is tender. Cool.

2 Peel away the aubergine skin, then place the flesh in a blender or food processor. Add the beef, onion, garlic, breadcrumbs, lemon zest, basil leaves and seasoning to taste and blend briefly. With wet hands, shape the mixture into 36 balls. Chill until ready to cook.

3 To make the sauce, heat the oil in a non-stick saucepan, add the bacon and onion and fry, stirring, for 3–4 minutes or until softened. Stir in the carrot, celery and garlic and fry, stirring frequently, for a further 5 minutes. Add the tomatoes with their juice, the wine and salt and pepper to taste. Bring to the boil, then reduce the heat, cover and simmer for 20 minutes.

4 While the sauce is cooking, fry the meatballs in a large non-stick frying pan without any fat. Fry in 3 batches, for 10–12 minutes each batch, until evenly browned and cooked through. As they are done, remove the meatballs with a draining spoon and drain on kitchen paper. When they are all cooked, add them to the sauce together with the chopped basil and keep warm.

5 Drop the tagliatelle into a large saucepan of boiling water. When the water returns to the boil, cook for 10–12 minutes, or according to the packet instructions, until al dente. Drain the pasta, toss with the meatballs and sauce and garnish with fresh basil leaves. Serve immediately.

Plus points

• Pasta made with egg (pasta all'uova) is a most valuable food, low in fat yet rich in protein, vitamins and minerals. It is also an excellent source of starchy carbohydrate, which is why it is favoured by athletes, especially the night before a big sporting event. When pasta is eaten, the starch is broken down into glucose. This is then stored in the muscles as glycogen, which is slowly released to provide energy during exercise.

• Adding aubergine and breadcrumbs to meatballs not only gives them a lovely flavour and light texture but it also increases the amount of fibre they contain.

• Frying the meatballs without any fat or oil draws out some of the fat in the beef, which can then be drained off and discarded.

Some more ideas

- Omit the basil and add 1 tbsp pesto to the sauce. Red pesto is particularly good.
- Stir 85 g (3 oz) baby leaf spinach into the sauce with the meatballs.
- Lean minced venison, lamb or pork can be used in place of the beef.
- If you like a spicy sauce, add ½ tsp chilli sauce or a few drops of Tabasco sauce.

- Use other pasta shapes – spaghetti and penne are also good with meatballs.
- Instead of celery use ½ bulb fennel, chopped.
- Serve the pasta topped with shavings of fresh Parmesan.
- The meatball mixture can also be shaped into patties and pan-fried in a little olive oil, then served inside burger buns with salad and tomato chutney.

Each serving provides

kcal 545, protein 28 g, fat 18 g (of which saturated fat 6 g), carbohydrate 68 g (of which sugars 8 g), fibre 5 g

✓✓✓	B_1, B_6, B_{12}, C, E, niacin
✓✓	A, folate, copper, potassium
✓	B_2, selenium

Shepherd's pie

In this version of a long-time family favourite, the minced lamb filling contains lots of vegetables and red lentils, giving a rich flavour and texture. A generous serving of peas will make the meal even more nutritious.

Serves 4

1 tbsp extra virgin olive oil

450 g (1 lb) lean minced lamb

1 large onion, finely chopped

3 carrots, finely chopped

3 celery sticks, thinly sliced

2 leeks, thinly sliced

1 tbsp tomato purée

1 tbsp Worcestershire sauce

360 ml (12 fl oz) lamb or beef stock, preferably home-made (see page 27)

100 g (3½ oz) split red lentils

3 tbsp chopped parsley

parsley sprigs to garnish

Potato and parsnip topping

500 g (1 lb 2 oz) floury potatoes, peeled and cut into chunks

500 g (1 lb 2 oz) parsnips, cut into chunks

75 ml (2½ fl oz) semi-skimmed milk

25 g (scant 1 oz) butter

salt and pepper

Preparation time: 45 minutes

Cooking time: 20 minutes

Each serving provides

kcal 570, **protein** 37 g, **fat** 20 g (of which saturated fat 9 g), **carbohydrate** 64 g (of which sugars 20 g), **fibre** 13 g

✓✓✓	A, B$_1$, B$_6$, B$_{12}$, C, E, folate, niacin, potassium, zinc
✓✓	B$_2$, calcium, iron
✓	selenium

1 Heat the oil in a large heavy saucepan. Add the lamb and cook over a high heat, stirring well with a wooden spoon to break up the meat, for about 5 minutes or until lightly browned. Push the meat to one side of the pan and add the onion. Reduce the heat to low and cook for 10 minutes, stirring occasionally, until the onion is softened and lightly browned.

2 Add the carrots, celery and leeks and stir well, then add the tomato purée, Worcestershire sauce, stock and lentils. Increase the heat and bring to the boil, stirring frequently. Partially cover with a lid, then reduce the heat to low and simmer for about 20 minutes, stirring occasionally.

3 While the meat mixture is cooking, preheat the oven to 200°C (400°F, gas mark 6) and prepare the topping. Place the potato and parsnip chunks in a saucepan and pour over boiling water to cover by 5 cm (2 in). Bring back to the boil, then reduce the heat and cook for 15–20 minutes or until the potatoes and parsnips are very tender. Heat the milk in a small saucepan until hot.

4 Drain the potatoes and parsnips well, and return them to the pan. Pour the hot milk over them, then mash them until they are completely smooth. Beat in the butter and season with salt and pepper to taste.

5 Remove the meat mixture from the heat, add the chopped parsley and seasoning to taste and stir well. Spoon into a large ovenproof dish, about 2.6 litre (4½ pint) capacity. Top with the mashed vegetables, spreading in an even layer. Bake for 20 minutes or until bubbling and lightly browned. Serve hot, garnished with parsley sprigs.

Another idea

● Replace the lamb with lean minced venison or wild boar. Omit the leeks and stir 250 g (8½ oz) fresh or frozen peas into the meat mixture after it has simmered for 15 minutes. In the topping, replace the parsnips with celeriac.

Plus points

● Carrots provide vitamin A in the form of beta-carotene. Cooking carrots makes it easier for the body to absorb and use the beta-carotene on offer.

● This well-balanced dish of lean meat, vegetables and pulses provides plenty of soluble fibre, mainly from the lentils but also from the parsnips, carrots and leeks. Soluble fibre controls levels of cholesterol and sugar in the blood.

Pork and beans

This is a dish from the Eastern seaboard of America, where the pork and beans are traditionally simmered slowly in an earthenware casserole. It is the kind of dish that you can prepare ahead and leave to bubble away while you tend to other things. Baked jacket potatoes and crusty bread are perfect for soaking up the delicious sauce.

Serves 4

250 g (8½ oz) dried white haricot beans, soaked overnight in cold water

1 tbsp sunflower oil

4 thin lean pork chump chops, about 625 g (1 lb 6 oz) in total, trimmed of fat

1 onion, chopped

250 ml (8½ fl oz) beer, such as dark ale

1 can chopped tomatoes, about 400 g

2 tsp Worcestershire sauce, or to taste

2 tbsp dark soft brown sugar

3 allspice berries

2 tbsp mild American or French mustard

2 smoked lean back bacon rashers, rinded and cut into bite-sized pieces

1 tsp cider vinegar, or to taste

Preparation time: 25 minutes, plus overnight soaking

Cooking time: about 2 hours

Each serving provides

kcal 490, protein 51 g, fat 11 g (of which saturated fat 3 g), carbohydrate 46 g (of which sugars 16 g), fibre 12 g

✓✓✓	B_1, B_2, B_6, B_{12}, E, niacin, iron, zinc
✓✓	C, calcium
✓	folate

1 Drain and rinse the beans, then place them in a large saucepan and pour over enough cold water to come up to about twice the depth of the beans. Cover the pan with its lid and bring to the boil. Skim off any scum, then reduce the heat, cover the pan again and cook the beans over a low heat for 45–60 minutes or until they are just tender.

2 Meanwhile, heat the oil in a deep flameproof casserole, add the pork chops and onion, and fry until the chops are browned on both sides. Pour in the beer and tomatoes with their juice, then add the Worcestershire sauce, sugar and allspice. Reduce the heat, cover and cook for about 1 hour or until the meat is very tender.

3 Drain the beans and add to the pork chops. Add the mustard, bacon and vinegar and stir well to mix. Cook, covered, over a low heat for a further hour or until both the beans and the pork are meltingly tender.

4 Before serving, taste for seasoning and add a dash or two more Worcestershire sauce or vinegar if liked.

Some more ideas

• Lager or cider can be used instead of beer.

• Instead of soaking and cooking dried beans, add a can of cannellini beans, about 400 g, drained and rinsed, at the beginning of step 3.

• Make Tuscan-style beans with sausages. Use 500 g (1 lb 2 oz) high-meat-content sausages, cut into bite-sized pieces, instead of the pork chops. Brown the sausages with the onion in a deep, non-stick frying pan; set aside. Pour off fat from the pan, then add 125 ml (4½ fl oz) red wine, 200 ml (7 fl oz) vegetable stock, 1 can chopped tomatoes, about 400 g, with the juice, 8 chopped fresh sage leaves, 2 bay leaves, 2 crushed garlic cloves and salt and pepper to taste. Cook uncovered over a low heat for 30 minutes. Add the sausages and onion together with 1 can cannellini beans, about 400 g, drained and rinsed, and simmer for 15 minutes.

Plus points

• Tomatoes contain lycopene, a carotenoid compound and a valuable antioxidant that is thought to protect against prostate, bladder and pancreatic cancers. Lycopene is enhanced by cooking and so is most readily available in processed tomato products, such as canned tomatoes, tomato purée and passata, and tomato ketchup.

Tender beef with oyster sauce

Stir-fries are a simple way to incorporate a variety of meat, vegetables and grains into your diet in one dish. Here, thin slices of rump steak team with egg-fried rice and colourful red pepper and broccoli to make a delicious combination of textures and flavours.

Serves 4

2 tbsp sunflower oil

300 g (10½ oz) lean rump steak, trimmed of fat and cut across the grain into thin slices

1 garlic clove, thinly sliced

2.5 cm (1 in) piece fresh root ginger, cut into fine shreds

2 red onions, cut into wedges

1 large red pepper, seeded and sliced

200 g (7 oz) small broccoli florets

6 tbsp oyster sauce

fresh coriander leaves to garnish

Egg-fried rice

225 g (8 oz) long-grain rice

1 tbsp sunflower oil

4 spring onions, sliced diagonally

100 g (3½ oz) frozen petit pois

2 eggs, beaten

1 tbsp light soy sauce

Preparation and cooking time: 45 minutes

Each serving provides

kcal 534, **protein** 31 g, **fat** 16 g (of which saturated fat 3 g), **carbohydrate** 70 g (of which sugars 12 g), **fibre** 6 g

✓✓✓	A, B₁, B₆, B₁₂, C, E, folate, niacin, zinc
✓✓	B₂, iron, selenium
✓	calcium

1 First cook the rice in a saucepan of boiling water for 10–12 minutes, or according to the packet instructions, until tender. Drain the rice well if necessary, return it to the pan, cover and keep hot.

2 Heat a wok or heavy-based frying pan until hot, add 1 tbsp of the oil and swirl to coat the wok. Add the beef, garlic and ginger and stir-fry for 2 minutes or until the beef is browned all over. Remove from the wok with a draining spoon and set aside.

3 Heat the remaining 1 tbsp oil in the wok until hot, then add the red onions, red pepper and broccoli. Stir-fry for 2 minutes or until the onions begin to colour. Return the beef and its juices to the wok, then add the oyster sauce and simmer for 1 minute.

4 At the same time as you are cooking the beef and vegetables, heat the oil for the egg-fried rice in another wok or frying pan and add the spring onions and petit pois. Stir-fry for 1 minute, then pour in the eggs and soy sauce and continue stirring until the eggs begin to scramble. Add the rice and stir well to mix, then leave to cook gently for 1 minute.

5 Spoon the rice into bowls, top with the beef mixture and garnish with coriander leaves. Serve immediately.

Plus points

• Eggs are an excellent source of many nutrients, including protein and iron.

• Broccoli is packed with vitamins. It is an excellent source of the antioxidants beta-carotene and vitamin C. It also provides good amounts of the B vitamins niacin and B₆ and useful amounts of folate.

• Stir-frying keeps all the water-soluble vitamins and minerals from the vegetables in the dish rather than pouring them down the sink with the cooking water. It's also a very quick method of cooking, so there is minimal nutrient loss.

Another idea

• Use 300 g (10½ oz) thinly sliced boneless lean pork loin instead of beef. Stir-fry with the garlic and ginger plus ½ tsp crushed dried chillies. Remove from the pan, then add 1 large yellow pepper, seeded and cut into strips, 2 thinly sliced carrots and 8 thickly sliced spring onions. Stir-fry for 2 minutes, then return the meat to the pan. Add 1 bottle yellow bean sauce, about 160 g, 1 tbsp light soy sauce and 4 tbsp water and cook for 1 minute. Serve over rice or noodles.

family favourites

Irish stew

Traditional recipes for Irish stew use a tough, fatty cut of lamb and only potatoes, onions and herbs. This up-to-date version with lamb leg steaks is leaner, and more colourful with the addition of carrots, but still retains its comforting, homely flavour. An unusual but delicious accompaniment is grilled Little Gem lettuce hearts.

Serves 4

4 boneless lean lamb leg steaks, about 500 g (1 lb 2 oz) in total, trimmed of fat and each steak cut into 4 pieces

1 kg (2¼ lb) floury potatoes, peeled and thickly sliced

1 large onion, sliced

500 g (1 lb 2 oz) carrots, thickly sliced

2 tbsp chopped parsley

1 tsp fresh thyme leaves

1 tbsp snipped fresh chives

450 ml (15 fl oz) hot lamb or vegetable stock

salt and pepper

chopped fresh thyme and parsley to garnish

Preparation time: 20 minutes
Cooking time: about 2 hours 20 minutes

1 Preheat the oven to 160°C (325°F, gas mark 3). In a large casserole, make layers of the lamb, potatoes, onion and carrots, sprinkling each layer with parsley, thyme, chives, and salt and pepper to taste. Finish with a layer of potatoes, then pour over the stock.

2 Cover the casserole with a tight-fitting lid and place in the oven to cook for about 2 hours or until both the meat and vegetables feel tender when tested with a skewer.

3 Increase the oven temperature to 200°C (400°F, gas mark 6). Remove the casserole lid and cook for a further 20 minutes or until the potatoes on top are golden brown and crisp. Serve hot, sprinkled with more thyme and parsley.

Some more ideas

• Lamb best end of neck cutlets are traditional in Irish stew and you can use 8 of them if you like, but make sure they are well trimmed of fat before layering them in the casserole.

• If you want the cooking liquid to be slightly thickened, sprinkle 1 tbsp pearl barley between the first few layers along with the herbs.

• Use turnips instead of carrots.

• Add 125 g (4½ oz) whole small button mushrooms, layering them in the casserole with the onion and carrots.

• For a real taste of Ireland, replace half of the stock with Guinness.

Plus points

• Carrots are not traditional in Irish stew, but they are well worth including, both for their colour and flavour and from a nutritional point of view. They are beneficial because they provide vitamins A and C as well as potassium.

• The value of potatoes as a nutritious and satisfying food was recognised by the Ministry of Food during the Second World War. It took steps to ensure that potatoes were readily available and never rationed.

Each serving provides

kcal 508, **protein** 32 g, **fat** 19 g (of which saturated fat 8 g), **carbohydrate** 58 g (of which sugars 14 g), **fibre** 7 g

✓✓✓	A, B₁, B₆, B₁₂, C, E, folate, niacin, zinc
✓✓	B₂, copper
✓	calcium, iron

Beefburgers with beetroot relish

These home-made burgers are healthily lean and full of flavour. They're served with griddled onions, watercress and a fabulous beetroot relish in mini focaccia – or in brown or white bread rolls or burger buns if you prefer. With chunky oven chips (see 'Some More Ideas', right) and a mixed leaf salad, you have a great meal.

Serves 4

2 slices Granary bread, with crusts

4 tbsp dry white wine

450 g (1 lb) lean rump or chuck steak, trimmed of fat and cut into small chunks

5 shallots, finely chopped

3 garlic cloves, finely chopped

2 tsp extra virgin olive oil

2 medium-sized onions, cut into thick slices

4 mini garlic-and-herb or plain focaccia, about 55 g each

50 g (1¾ oz) watercress

salt and pepper

Beetroot and basil relish

2 cooked beetroot, vacuum-packed (not in vinegar), diced

12 fresh basil leaves, shredded

2 tsp extra virgin olive oil

dash of balsamic vinegar

Preparation and cooking time: about 40 minutes

Each serving provides

kcal 280, **protein** 31 g, **fat** 9 g (of which saturated fat 3 g), **carbohydrate** 18 g (of which sugars 8 g), **fibre** 3 g

✓✓✓	B$_1$, B$_6$, B$_{12}$, E, niacin, zinc
✓✓	B$_2$, folate
✓	A

1 Break the Granary bread into small pieces and place them in a bowl. Pour over the wine and set aside.

2 Mince the beef in a mincer or food processor. (If using a food processor, take care not to grind too fine.) Add the bread and mince or pulse for 30 seconds, then turn the mixture into a bowl. Add the shallots and garlic and season with salt and pepper to taste. Form into 4 burger shapes and chill until ready to cook.

3 To make the relish, put the diced beetroot and shredded basil in a bowl, sprinkle over the oil and balsamic vinegar, and season with salt and pepper to taste. Mix gently, then cover and chill until ready to serve.

4 Heat a ridged cast-iron grill pan or non-stick frying pan over a moderate heat until hot. Brush with a little of the olive oil, then add the sliced onions and cook for 6–8 minutes or until softened and lightly charred on both sides. Remove them from the pan and keep hot.

5 Brush the pan with a little more olive oil. Split the focaccia in half, then lightly toast the cut sides in the pan. Remove the bread to a plate. Brush the pan with oil again, then put in the burgers and cook over a moderately high heat for 3–4 minutes. Using a fish slice or spatula, carefully turn each burger over. Cook the second side for 3–4 minutes. Return the onions to the pan and cook with the burgers for a few more minutes to reheat.

6 Arrange a piece of focaccia, toasted side up, on each plate. Top with a burger and add some onions, beetroot relish and watercress. Cover with the remaining pieces of focaccia, toasted side down. Serve immediately.

Plus points

• Commercial burgers contain around 21% fat. This home-made burger contains only 11% fat and it is high in monounsaturates, the healthy kind of fat linked with the prevention of coronary heart disease.

• There are lots of onions in this dish, plus shallots and garlic. These are all alliums, members of the lily family, which contain a phytochemical called allicin. Allicin is believed to help lower blood cholesterol levels and stimulate the immune system.

family favourites

Some more ideas

• If you don't have a machine to mince the beef, you can buy rump or chuck steak and ask the butcher to mince it for you. Or chop the meat yourself using 2 chef's knives. The result will be coarser than mince made in a machine.

• Super-chunky oven chips are a great healthy alternative to deep-fried chips. Preheat the oven to 240ºC (475ºF, gas mark 9) and heat a roasting tin in the oven. Cut 4 scrubbed baking potatoes (with the skin) into big wedges and place them in a polythene bag. Add 1–2 tbsp sunflower oil or olive oil, 1–2 tsp dried parsley and seasoning to taste, then shake the bag to coat the potatoes. Tip them into the hot roasting tin and bake for 45–50 minutes, turning once or twice, until they are crisp and well browned on all sides. Serve immediately.

Bangers and mash

Venison is a particularly lean meat and makes a good flavoursome sausage, perfect for this sophisticated version of an all-time family favourite. Serve with broccoli florets or another seasonal green vegetable.

Serves 4

1 tbsp sunflower oil

8 large venison sausages, about 500 g
    (1 lb 2 oz) in total

170 g (6 oz) baby onions, halved

1 large garlic clove, crushed

170 g (6 oz) button mushrooms, halved

1 red pepper, seeded and thinly sliced

200 ml (7 fl oz) beef stock, preferably
    home-made (see page 27)

150 ml (5 fl oz) full-bodied red wine

1 tbsp redcurrant or bramble jelly

3 sprigs of fresh thyme

2 tsp cornflour

salt and pepper

Olive oil mash

750 g (1 lb 10 oz) floury potatoes, peeled and
    cut into chunks

120 ml (4 fl oz) semi-skimmed milk

2 tsp extra virgin olive oil

1 tbsp chopped parsley

Preparation and cooking time: 1½ hours

Each serving provides

kcal 666, **protein** 40 g, **fat** 33 g (of which saturated fat 11 g), **carbohydrate** 48 g (of which sugars 13 g), **fibre** 7 g

✓✓✓	B₁, B₆, B₁₂, C, E, folate, niacin
✓✓	A, potassium
✓	iron, selenium, zinc

1 Heat the oil in a deep non-stick frying pan. Add the sausages and fry them over a moderate heat, turning occasionally, for 10 minutes or until they are lightly browned all over.

2 Meanwhile, start cooking the potatoes for the mash. Place the potatoes in a saucepan and pour over boiling water to cover by 5 cm (2 in). Bring back to the boil, then reduce the heat and cook for 15–20 minutes or until the potatoes are very tender.

3 Add the onions to the sausages and cook for a further 5 minutes or until they are golden and the sausages are nicely browned all over. Remove the sausages to a plate and set aside. Drain off the excess oil from the pan.

4 Add the garlic, mushrooms and red pepper to the pan and cook gently for a few minutes until softened. Pour in the stock and wine and add the fruit jelly and 2 sprigs of thyme. Season with salt and pepper to taste. Mix the cornflour with 1 tbsp cold water and stir into the liquid in the pan. Bring to the boil, stirring until lightly thickened, then reduce the heat and return the sausages to the pan. Simmer gently for 10 minutes.

5 Drain the potatoes, shaking the colander or sieve to remove any excess water, and return them to their pan. Heat the milk in a small saucepan until hot, pour over the potatoes and mash until smooth. Beat in the oil, parsley and salt and pepper to taste.

6 To serve, divide the mash among warmed plates and top with the sausages, vegetables and sauce (discarding the thyme sprigs). Sprinkle with the leaves from the remaining thyme sprig and serve immediately.

Plus points

• Venison sausages contain just over half the amount of fat found in traditional pork sausages (11% fat compared with 20% fat on average). They also have a deeper, 'meatier' taste. The venison in the sausages provides valuable amounts of haem iron, the most easily absorbed form of iron.

• Red wine is rich in flavonoids, which can help to protect against heart disease and stroke. Cabernet Sauvignon, Merlot and Pinot Noir wines, particularly from Chile, have been shown to have higher levels of flavonoids than other wines.

Some more ideas

- If venison sausages are unavailable, use any good-quality, high-meat-content sausages.
- Turn this dish into something special for informal entertaining by using wild boar sausages, apples and cranberries. Shallow-fry the sausages in 1 tbsp oil, turning them frequently until evenly browned. Add the onions and cook as in the main recipe, then remove the sausages and onions and pour off the oil from the pan. Add 150 ml (5 fl oz) each dry cider and beef stock with 2 thickly sliced dessert apples, 2 tsp wholegrain mustard, 2 tbsp cranberry jelly and the grated zest of ½ orange. Bring to the boil, then reduce the heat and return the sausages and onions to the pan. Cook gently for 10 minutes. Add 125 g (4½ oz) fresh or frozen cranberries, stir and cook gently for 5 minutes or until the fruit is just tender. Thicken the sauce with the cornflour as in the main recipe, then serve.

Keema curry

This mellow curry has just a hint of chilli, so it's ideal for children who like to be a little adventurous with their food. Serve with steamed basmati rice and warm naan bread.

Serves 4

500 g (1 lb 2 oz) lean minced beef

1 onion, finely chopped

450 g (1 lb) potatoes, peeled and diced

3 garlic cloves, chopped

2.5 cm (1 in) piece fresh root ginger, peeled and finely chopped

1 cinnamon stick, halved

1 tsp turmeric

1 tsp cumin seeds, roughly crushed

1 tsp coriander seeds, roughly crushed

½ tsp crushed dried chillies

1 can chopped tomatoes, about 400 g

300 ml (10 fl oz) beef or lamb stock, preferably home-made (see page 27)

150 g (5½ oz) baby leaf spinach

salt and pepper

fresh mint leaves to garnish

Raita

150 g (5½ oz) plain low-fat yogurt

¼ cucumber, finely diced

4 tsp chopped fresh mint

Preparation time: 10–15 minutes

Cooking time: 35 minutes

Each serving provides

kcal 369, **protein** 35 g, **fat** 14 g (of which saturated fat 6 g), **carbohydrate** 30 g (of which sugars 10 g), **fibre** 4 g

---

✓✓✓ B_1, B_6, B_{12}, C, E, folate, iron, zinc

✓✓ A, B_2

---

1 Fry the beef and onion in a large saucepan for 5 minutes or until evenly browned, stirring to break up the meat. Add the potatoes, garlic, ginger and spices and fry for 2 minutes, stirring. Add the tomatoes with their juice and the stock and season with salt and pepper to taste. Bring to the boil, then cover and simmer for 20 minutes, stirring occasionally.

2 Meanwhile, make the raita. Mix the yogurt, cucumber and mint together with a little seasoning. Spoon into a small bowl and chill until required.

3 Stir the spinach into the curry and heat through for 1 minute, then taste for seasoning. Spoon the curry onto warmed plates and sprinkle with fresh mint leaves. Serve immediately, with the chilled raita.

Some more ideas

● If you prefer, you can cook the curry in the oven. Brown the beef and onion in a flameproof casserole, then add the other ingredients and bring to the boil. Cover and cook in a preheated 180°C (350°F, gas mark 4) oven for 1 hour. Add the spinach, toss with the meat, then cover and return to the oven to cook for 10 minutes.

● If you don't have the individual dried spices, you can use 2 tbsp mild curry paste instead.

● Use Swiss chard or spring greens in place of the spinach. Tear into bite-sized pieces before adding to the meat.

● For a fruity curry, add 55 g (2 oz) sultanas and 1 sliced dessert apple with the potatoes. Omit the spinach. Garnish the curry with 1 diced banana tossed with the juice of ½ lemon, 2 tbsp chopped fresh coriander and 2 tbsp toasted desiccated coconut.

● Any leftover curry is delicious reheated and served in folded chapattis or warmed pitta bread pockets.

● To vary the raita, add ½ grated carrot, 2 chopped spring onions or a sprinkling of toasted cumin seeds to the basic mixture.

● If you don't have any fresh mint, use 1½ tsp ready-made mint sauce instead.

Plus points

● A raita or sauce of yogurt, cucumber and mint is often served with curries to act as a cooling agent against the heat of the chillies and spices. Yogurt is also extremely nutritious – it is a valuable source of calcium and it provides useful amounts of phosphorus and vitamins B_2 and B_{12}. Live yogurt also provides beneficial bacteria that can help to maintain a healthy digestive tract.

Sweet and sour pork

Sweet and sour sauce doesn't have to be thick, gloopy and bright orange. This modern, light version allows the succulence of the meat and the fresh flavours and different textures of a colourful variety of vegetables and noodles to shine through. Some plainly cooked rice is all that is needed to complete the meal.

Serves 4

340 g (12 oz) pork fillet (tenderloin), trimmed of fat and cut into 5 x 1 cm (2 x ½ in) strips

1 tbsp light soy sauce

2 tsp cornflour

2 sheets medium Chinese egg noodles, about 125 g (4½ oz) in total

2 tbsp sunflower oil

8 baby corn, about 75 g (2½ oz) in total, quartered lengthways

170 g (6 oz) carrots, cut into fine shreds about 5 cm (2 in) long

1 large garlic clove, finely chopped

1 tbsp finely diced fresh root ginger

300 g (10½ oz) bean sprouts

4 spring onions, sliced diagonally

1 tsp toasted sesame oil

pepper

Sweet and sour sauce

1 tbsp cornflour

1 tbsp demerara sugar

1 tbsp rice wine vinegar

2 tbsp rice wine or dry sherry

2 tbsp tomato ketchup

3 tbsp light soy sauce

1 can pineapple slices in natural juice, about 425 g, drained and chopped, with juice reserved

Preparation time: 35 minutes
Cooking time: 15 minutes

1 Place the pork strips in a bowl, sprinkle over the soy sauce and pepper to taste and stir to coat the meat. Sprinkle over the cornflour and stir again. Cover and set aside.

2 To make the sauce, mix together the cornflour, sugar, vinegar, rice wine or sherry, ketchup, soy sauce and reserved pineapple juice in a small bowl. Set aside.

3 Cook the noodles in a saucepan of boiling water for 3 minutes, or cook or soak them according to the packet instructions. Drain well and set aside.

4 Heat a wok or heavy-based frying pan until really hot, then add 1 tbsp of the oil and swirl to coat the wok. Add the pork and leave for 1 minute to brown, then stir-fry over a high heat for 3–4 minutes. Remove the pork with a draining spoon and set aside.

5 Heat the remaining oil in the wok, then add the corn and stir-fry for 1 minute. Add the carrots, garlic and ginger and stir-fry for another minute. Sprinkle over 5 tbsp water and let the vegetables steam for 2–3 minutes.

6 Pour in the sauce mixture, stir well and bring to the boil. Put the meat back in the wok and add the noodles, pineapple and bean sprouts. Heat through, stirring and tossing. Add the spring onions and sesame oil and serve.

Some more ideas

• For a hotter sauce, add 1 small fresh red chilli, seeded and finely chopped.

• For a sweeter sauce, use 1 can pineapple slices in syrup, about 425 g, or add a little more demerara sugar.

• Use boneless pork shoulder instead of fillet.

Plus points

• Over the last 20 years, farmers have been breeding leaner pigs, and pork now contains considerably less fat than it did in the past. The average fat content is much the same as skinless chicken breast.

• Bean sprouts are rich in vitamin C and several of the B vitamins; they also provide some potassium. Adding them at the last minute preserves as much of their vitamin C content as possible.

Each serving provides

kcal 369, **protein** 25 g, **fat** 11 g (of which saturated fat 2 g), **carbohydrate** 45 g (of which sugars 26 g), **fibre** 4 g

✓✓✓	A, B$_1$, B$_6$, B$_{12}$, C, E, folate, niacin
✓✓	B$_2$, iron, zinc
✓	selenium

Spinach-stuffed meatloaf

Vegetables and oats make this meatloaf wonderfully moist and light. When sliced, the creamy spinach layer is revealed in a pretty spiral. Serve with roasted mixed vegetables such as potatoes, courgettes and red onions.

Serves 6

1 tbsp extra virgin olive oil
2 large onions, finely chopped
6 garlic cloves, crushed, or to taste
1 can chopped tomatoes, about 400 g
150 ml (5 fl oz) chicken stock
1 tsp dried mixed herbs
500 g (1 lb 2 oz) young spinach leaves
2 tbsp crème fraîche
½ tsp freshly grated nutmeg
450 g (1 lb) lean minced beef
450 g (1 lb) lean minced pork
1 celery stick, finely chopped
1 large carrot, grated
50 g (1¾ oz) porridge oats
2 tsp chopped fresh thyme
5 tbsp semi-skimmed milk
1 egg, beaten
2 tsp Dijon mustard
salt and pepper

Preparation time: 45 minutes, plus 10 minutes standing
Cooking time: 50 minutes

Each serving provides

kcal 340, **protein** 40 g, **fat** 14 g (of which saturated fat 4 g), **carbohydrate** 19 g (of which sugars 11 g), **fibre** 5 g

✓✓✓	A, B₁, B₆, B₁₂, C, E, niacin, zinc
✓✓	B₂, calcium, selenium
✓	iron

1 Heat the oil in a saucepan over a moderate heat. Add the onions and garlic and cook, stirring frequently, for about 5 minutes or until the onions are soft and golden.

2 Transfer half of the onion mixture to a large bowl and set aside. Stir the tomatoes with their juice, the stock and mixed herbs into the onions remaining in the saucepan. Season with salt and pepper to taste. Bring to the boil, then cover and leave to simmer very gently, stirring occasionally, while preparing the meatloaf.

3 Preheat the oven to 180°C (350°F, gas mark 4). Wash the spinach and put it in a large saucepan. Cover with a tight-fitting lid and cook over a high heat for 2–3 minutes, shaking the pan frequently, until the leaves are wilted.

4 Tip the spinach into a colander to drain. When it is cool enough to handle, squeeze it dry with your hands, then chop it roughly and put it into a bowl. Stir in the crème fraîche and season with half of the nutmeg and salt and pepper to taste.

5 Put the beef and pork into the bowl with the reserved onion. Add the celery, carrot, porridge oats, thyme, milk, egg, mustard and remaining ¼ tsp nutmeg. Season with salt and pepper to taste. Mix the ingredients very well together with your hands.

6 Lay a large sheet of cling film on the work surface and place the meat mixture in the centre. With a palette knife, spread the meat into a 23 x 18 cm (9 x 7 in) rectangle. Spread the spinach mixture evenly over the meat, leaving a 1 cm (½ in) border all round. Starting at a short end, carefully roll up the meat and spinach like a Swiss roll, using the cling film to help. Pat the sides into a neat shape and place the roll on a non-stick baking tray, discarding the cling film.

7 Place the meatloaf, uncovered, in the centre of the oven and cook for 45 minutes, then remove from the oven and brush lightly all over with a little of the tomato sauce. Return to the oven and cook for 5 minutes to set the glaze and brown it slightly. To check if the meatloaf is cooked right through, insert a skewer into the centre and remove after a few seconds – it should feel very hot when lightly placed on the back of your hand.

8 When the meatloaf is ready, remove it from the oven, cover loosely with foil and leave to stand for 10 minutes. Serve cut into slices, with the rest of the tomato sauce.

Plus points

- Spinach provides good amounts of several antioxidants, including vitamins C and E. It also offers carotenoid compounds and substantial amounts of the B vitamins, including folate, niacin and B_6.
- Porridge oats are an excellent source of soluble fibre which can help to reduce high blood cholesterol levels.

Some more ideas

- Minced beef can be used on its own for a more traditional meatloaf, or you can use minced turkey, chicken or veal instead of either the beef or the pork. You could also use a combination of three different meats.
- Leftover meatloaf is delicious sliced and served cold with salad or in sandwiches.
- For 2 meatloaf and potato pies, each serving 4, make the meatloaf mixture as in the main recipe, but use 900 g (2 lb) spinach and 4 tbsp crème fraîche or soured cream for the spinach filling. Cook 1.5 kg (3 lb 3 oz) peeled potatoes in boiling water until tender; mash with enough milk to make a light fluffy texture and season with salt and pepper to taste. Divide the meat mixture in half and press into two 23 cm (9 in) springform tins. Top each with half of the spinach, spreading it into an even layer, then cover with the mashed potatoes. Set the tins on baking trays and bake in a preheated 180ºC (350ºF, gas mark 4) oven for 55 minutes. Let stand for 10 minutes, then remove the sides of the tins and serve the pies cut into wedges.

Chilli con carne with cornbread

Slow-cooked beef and beans in a rich tomato sauce spiced with chillies and cumin makes an inviting meal on a wintry day, and warm, crumbly-moist cornbread studded with sweetcorn kernels and mild green chilli is the perfect accompaniment. Serve with a crisp salad for a hearty, well-balanced meal.

Serves 6

1 tbsp extra virgin olive oil

340 g (12 oz) lean stewing beef, trimmed of fat and cut into small cubes

1 large onion, finely chopped

2 garlic cloves, crushed

½ tsp cumin seeds

1 tsp crushed dried chillies, or to taste

1 tbsp tomato purée

1 can chopped tomatoes, about 400 g

2 cans red kidney beans, about 400 g each, drained and rinsed

300 ml (10 fl oz) beef stock, preferably home-made (see page 27)

salt and pepper

Cornbread

140 g (5 oz) cornmeal

115 g (4 oz) plain flour

2 tsp baking powder

½ tsp salt

1 large egg

225 ml (7½ fl oz) semi-skimmed milk

140 g (5 oz) fresh sweetcorn kernels or thawed frozen sweetcorn kernels

1 small mild fresh green chilli, seeded and finely chopped

Preparation time: 25 minutes

Cooking time: 1–1½ hours

1 Heat the oil in a large flameproof casserole, add the beef and fry over a high heat, stirring occasionally, for 3–4 minutes or until well browned. Remove the meat with a draining spoon.

2 Reduce the heat to low and add the onion to the pan. Stir well and cook gently for 10 minutes. Add the garlic, cumin seeds and chillies and cook, stirring, for 1 minute, then return the meat to the pan. Add the tomato purée, the tomatoes with their juice, the beans and stock. Stir well and bring to the boil. Reduce the heat so the chilli is simmering gently, then cover with a lid and cook for 1–1½ hours or until the meat is tender, stirring occasionally.

3 Meanwhile, make the cornbread. Preheat the oven to 200°C (400°F, gas mark 6) and grease a shallow 20 cm (8 in) square cake tin with a little melted butter. Mix the cornmeal, flour, baking powder and salt in a bowl. Combine the egg with the milk and stir in to make a thick, rough-looking batter (do not overmix or the bread will be tough). Fold in the sweetcorn and chilli. Spoon into the prepared tin and bake for 20–25 minutes until firm to the touch.

4 Turn the cornbread out of its tin and cut into large squares. Serve the chilli in warmed bowls, with the warm cornbread.

Plus points

● Red kidney beans are low in fat and rich in carbohydrate. They provide good amounts of vitamins B_1, niacin and B_6, and useful amounts of iron. They are also a good source of soluble fibre, which can help to reduce high cholesterol levels in the blood.

● Sweetcorn and cornmeal (milled from maize) are good sources of complex (starchy) carbohydrates.

Each serving provides

kcal 408, **protein** 28 g, **fat** 8 g (of which saturated fat 2 g), **carbohydrate** 59 g (of which sugars 10 g), **fibre** 8 g

✓✓✓	B_1, B_6, B_{12}, E, niacin, zinc
✓✓	B_2, C, folate, calcium, iron, selenium
✓	A

Some more ideas

• Replace the beef with diced boneless lean lamb (leg or neck fillet). Replace the crushed chillies with 1 seeded and finely chopped medium-hot fresh green chilli, ½ tsp ground coriander and 1 cinnamon stick. Instead of kidney beans, use 2 cans chickpeas, about 400 g each, drained and rinsed, adding them to the casserole after the chilli has been cooking for 15 minutes. Also add 2 medium-sized aubergines, cut into 1 cm (½ in) dice. Stir occasionally and add more stock if the mixture looks dry. At the end of the cooking time, stir in 3 tbsp chopped fresh coriander.

• Instead of serving with cornbread, mix 150 g (5½ oz) coarse fresh breadcrumbs with 1 seeded and finely chopped small, mild, fresh green chilli and scatter over the top of the chilli. Bake in a preheated 220ºC (425ºF, gas mark 7) oven for about 15 minutes or until the topping is crisp and golden.

Spring lamb and vegetable stew

Based on a classic French dish called *navarin*, this is a delectable stew. In France it is made in the spring, as a celebration of the new season's lamb and the delicate young vegetables. Serve with a dish of freshly cooked spring greens, and hand round a basket of crusty French bread.

Serves 4

2 tbsp extra virgin olive oil

1 large onion, chopped

1 garlic clove, finely chopped

450 g (1 lb) lean boneless leg of lamb, trimmed of fat and cut into cubes

150 ml (5 fl oz) dry white wine

450 ml (15 fl oz) lamb or chicken stock

1 bay leaf

1 sprig of fresh thyme

900 g (2 lb) baby new potatoes, scrubbed

225 g (8 oz) baby carrots

150 g (5½ oz) button onions

200 g (7 oz) small turnips, diced

250 g (8½ oz) shelled fresh peas or 125 g (4½ oz) frozen peas

2 tbsp chopped parsley

salt and pepper

Preparation time: 30 minutes

Cooking time: 1¾–2 hours

1 Preheat the oven to 180°C (350°F, gas mark 4). Heat the oil in a large flameproof casserole, add the chopped onion and garlic and cook, stirring, for 5 minutes or until softened. Add the cubes of lamb and cook for 5 minutes or until browned on all sides, stirring so they colour evenly.

2 Add the wine, stock, bay leaf, thyme, potatoes, carrots and button onions. Season with salt and pepper to taste. Bring to the boil, then cover with a tight-fitting lid and transfer to the oven. Cook for 1 hour.

3 Add the turnips and stir. Cover again and continue cooking for 30–45 minutes or until the meat and vegetables are tender, adding the peas 10 minutes before the end of the cooking time.

4 Add the parsley and stir well. Taste and add more salt and pepper if needed. Serve hot.

Some more ideas

● For a lamb stew with a Provençal flavour, use red wine instead of white. Omit the stock and add 1 can chopped tomatoes, about 400 g, with the juice, and a large sprig of fresh rosemary. When you add the peas, also stir in 50 g (1¾ oz) stoned black olives.

● Mange-tout or French beans can be used instead of the peas.

Each serving provides

kcal 495, **protein** 31 g, **fat** 16 g (of which saturated fat 5 g), **carbohydrate** 52 g (of which sugars 14 g), **fibre** 8 g

✓✓✓	A, B_1, B_6, B_{12}, C, E, folate, niacin, zinc
✓✓	iron
✓	B_2, selenium

Plus points

● Peas provide good amounts of the B vitamins B_1, niacin and B_6. They also provide dietary fibre, particularly the soluble variety, some folate and vitamin C. Frozen vegetables are just as nutritious as fresh vegetables, and in many cases they have been shown to contain higher levels of vitamin C.

● In addition to providing fibre, turnips contain the B vitamins niacin and B_6, and are a useful source of vitamin C.

family favourites

93

Toad-in-the-hole

Sausages without skins are simple to prepare, and you know what goes into them when you make them yourself. Here home-made pork sausages flavoured with sun-dried tomatoes and leeks are cooked in a herby batter, then served with mashed root vegetables and home-made baked beans for a satisfying healthy meal.

Serves 4

300 g (10½ oz) lean minced pork

100 g (3½ oz) fresh breadcrumbs

1 medium-sized leek, about 150 g (5½ oz), finely chopped

55 g (2 oz) soft (*mi-cuit*) sun-dried tomatoes, chopped

2 tbsp sunflower oil

salt and pepper

Batter

125 g (4½ oz) plain flour

2 eggs

300 ml (10 fl oz) semi-skimmed milk

2 tbsp chopped parsley

Root vegetable mash

2 medium-sized carrots, about 225 g (8 oz) in total, cut into chunks

2 medium-sized parsnips, about 400 g (14 oz) in total, cut into chunks

1 swede, about 400 g (14 oz), cut into chunks

200 g (7 oz) French beans, trimmed and sliced diagonally

Baked beans

1 small red onion, finely chopped

1 garlic clove, crushed

3 tbsp tomato purée

200 ml (7 fl oz) vegetable stock

2 cans cannellini beans, about 400 g each, drained and rinsed

Preparation and cooking time: 1¼ hours

1 Preheat the oven to 220°C (425°F, gas mark 7). To make the sausages, combine the pork, breadcrumbs, leek and sun-dried tomatoes in a bowl and season to taste. Mix well, then shape into 8 sausages, each about 10 x 2.5cm (4 x 1 in). Place on a plate and chill.

2 For the batter, sift the flour and a pinch of salt into a bowl. Make a well in the centre and add the eggs and half the milk. Whisk, gradually incorporating the flour to make a thick lump-free batter. Slowly whisk in the remaining milk to make a smooth thin batter, then whisk in the parsley.

3 Put the oil in a 30 x 25 cm (12 x 10 in) non-stick roasting tin and heat in the oven for 5 minutes. Add the sausages and cook for 10 minutes. Remove the tin from the oven. Stir the batter, then pour it over the sausages. Return the tin to the oven and cook for 30 minutes or until the batter is crisp and golden brown.

4 Meanwhile put the carrots, parsnips and swede in a saucepan and pour over boiling water to cover them by 5 cm (2 in). Bring back to the boil, then simmer for 20 minutes or until the vegetables are very tender.

5 Combine all the ingredients for the baked beans in a large saucepan and bring to the boil. Cook for about 10 minutes or until thickened. Keep hot. At the same time, steam the French beans for about 3 minutes or until they are just tender.

6 Drain the root vegetables well. Return them to the pan and mash until they are completely smooth, then stir in the French beans and seasoning.

7 Serve the toad-in-the-hole hot, with the mashed root vegetables and baked beans alongside.

Plus points

• This is an excellent meal for growing children and teenagers because it contains such a variety of nutrients. The pork provides protein and zinc. The eggs provide protein, iron, zinc, selenium and vitamins A, B and E, while the milk provides protein, calcium, phosphorus and many of the B vitamins. Between them, the vegetables supply vitamins A, B, C and E.

• In these days of refrigerated transport and all-year-round variety, it is easy to forget the importance of root vegetables, such as parsnips and swede, as a source of vitamin C. At one time, these vegetables were very important in preventing scurvy in Britain during the winter months.

Some more ideas
● For extra iron, replace the pork with lean minced venison, and substitute ready-to-eat dried apricots for the sun-dried tomatoes.

● If you can't get *mi-cuit* tomatoes, use sun-dried tomatoes in oil and drain them well.

● Instead of the root vegetable mash and baked beans, serve the toad-in-the-hole with baked potatoes and crisp stir-fried vegetables. Use 200 g (7 oz) sugarsnap peas, and 2 courgettes and 3 carrots, all sliced on the diagonal. Heat a wok until hot, then add 1 tbsp sunflower oil and swirl to coat the wok. Add the vegetables and stir-fry over a high heat for 2 minutes. Pour in 3 tbsp vegetable stock and 1 tbsp soy sauce, reduce the heat to moderate and stir-fry for 3–5 minutes or until the vegetables are tender but still slightly crunchy.

Each serving provides
kcal 800, **protein** 46 g, **fat** 25 g (of which saturated fat 5 g), **carbohydrate** 106 g (of which sugars 78 g), **fibre** 25 g

✓✓✓ A, B₁, B₂, B₆, B₁₂, C, E, niacin, calcium, iron, zinc

✓✓ selenium

Weekend Meals

Meaty treats when there's more time to spare

A good, old-fashioned roast will never go out of fashion, and it's easy to cook it the healthy way. Try tender roast beef British-style with Yorkshire puddings and all the trimmings – or break with tradition and roast leg of lamb the French way with garlic and beans, or pork as the Germans like it, with fruit and ginger. Casseroles and stews are always popular for weekend meals, and your family and friends will be sure to enjoy New England simmered beef served with a tangy beetroot relish, or pork cooked slowly with apples and cider. For warmer weather there are lamb kebabs on figgy rice or meat-stuffed baked vegetables Mediterranean-style.

Sunday special roast beef

Succulent roast beef, crispy roast potatoes and root vegetables, and feather-light Yorkshire puddings make one of the best loved of Sunday lunches. This healthy version will please everyone, even the traditionalists.

Serves 8

1.5 kg (3 lb 3 oz) boned, rolled and tied lean sirloin of beef, trimmed of fat

4 tsp made English mustard (optional)

450 ml (15 fl oz) beef stock, preferably home-made (see page 27)

salt and pepper

Yorkshire puddings

50 g (1¾ oz) plain flour

1 egg

100 ml (3½ fl oz) semi-skimmed milk

2 tsp sunflower oil

Roast vegetables

1.35 kg (3 lb) floury potatoes, peeled and cut into even-sized pieces

675 g (1½ lb) baby parsnips, halved lengthways

675 g (1½ lb) baby carrots, halved lengthways

3 tbsp sunflower oil

675 g (1½ lb) broccoli florets

Preparation and cooking time: 2¼–2¾ hours

Each serving provides

kcal 514, **protein** 53 g, **fat** 13 g (of which saturated fat 5 g), **carbohydrate** 51 g (of which sugars 11 g), **fibre** 8 g

✓✓✓	A, B₁, B₂, B₆, B₁₂, C, E, folate, niacin, potassium, zinc
✓✓	iron, selenium
✓	calcium

1 Preheat the oven to 180°C (350°F, gas mark 4). Weigh the joint of beef and calculate the cooking time (see page 22).

2 Put the meat, fat side uppermost, on a rack in a roasting tin. Season with pepper, then spread with 3 tsp of the mustard, if using. Roast the meat in the oven for the calculated time, basting occasionally with the juices in the tin.

3 Meanwhile, prepare the Yorkshire pudding batter. In a bowl, mix together the flour and a pinch of salt. Make a well in the centre and add the egg. Add a little of the milk and beat together, gradually beginning to work in the flour. Slowly beat in the remaining milk and 4 tbsp water, until all the flour is incorporated and the batter is smooth. Set aside.

4 Next prepare the vegetables. Put the potatoes in a large saucepan of boiling water and boil for 5 minutes. Drain well and return to the pan, then cover and shake vigorously to roughen the surface of the potatoes (this helps to make them crisp).

5 Put the parsnips and carrots in another large saucepan of boiling water and boil for 3 minutes, then drain.

6 One hour before the end of the roasting time for the beef, put 2 tbsp of the oil in a non-stick roasting tin and the remaining 1 tbsp oil in another non-stick roasting tin. Heat on top of the cooker, then add the potatoes to the 2 tbsp oil and the parsnips and carrots to the 1 tbsp oil. Baste each piece of vegetable with oil, then quickly place the tins in the oven with the beef. (With a gas oven, put the potatoes above the meat and the vegetables below.) After 30 minutes, turn the potatoes and vegetables so they will crisp and brown evenly.

7 When the beef is cooked, remove it from the oven and increase the heat to 220°C (425°F, gas mark 7). Place the beef on a warmed plate, cover with foil and keep warm. Divide the oil for the Yorkshire puddings among 12 non-stick patty tins and put in the top of the oven to heat for 2–3 minutes. (Move the potatoes down a shelf.) Stir the batter, pour it into the tins and bake for 15 minutes or until the puddings are risen and golden brown.

8 Meanwhile, steam the broccoli for 10 minutes or until tender, and make the gravy: pour the fat very slowly from the roasting tin, leaving the sediment behind. Place the tin on top of the cooker and pour in the stock. Bring to the boil, stirring and scraping up all the browned cooking residue on the bottom of the tin, then simmer until slightly reduced. Season and stir in the remaining mustard, if using.

9 To serve, transfer the meat to a warmed serving platter and surround with the roast potatoes and root vegetables and the Yorkshire puddings. Put the broccoli in a warmed serving dish. Add any meat juices that have collected on the plate to the gravy and stir to combine, then skim off any fat. Pour the gravy into a gravy boat and serve immediately.

Plus points

• This recipe for a traditional favourite is the perfect example of a healthy well-balanced meal. Modest portions of protein (from the meat) are accompanied by lots of starchy carbohydrates and fresh vegetables. It's also healthily low in fat.

Some more ideas

• In true British style, serve the beef with a pot of mustard, the hotter the better. Alternatively, serve with horseradish sauce.

• Topside can be roasted instead of sirloin. It is leaner and less expensive than sirloin, but not quite so tender and flavoursome.

• Add more green vegetables. French or green beans and finely shredded Savoy cabbage are both delicious with roast beef.

weekend meals

Roast leg of lamb with beans

Lamb and flageolet beans are often served together in French country cooking because they complement each other so well. In this recipe the flageolets are mixed with potatoes and green beans, and the dish is deliciously flavoured with lemon, garlic and rosemary. Serve in true French style, with a crusty baguette.

Serves 6

250 g (8½ oz) dried flageolet beans, soaked overnight in cold water

4 large garlic cloves, peeled

1 bay leaf

900 g (2 lb) boneless lean leg of lamb, trimmed of fat

4 small sprigs of fresh rosemary

½ lemon, thinly sliced

3 tsp olive oil

675 g (1½ lb) floury potatoes, peeled and cut into 2.5 cm (1 in) cubes

2 shallots, finely chopped

4 tomatoes, diced

4 tbsp chopped parsley

450 g (1 lb) green beans

4 tbsp red wine

300 ml (10 fl oz) lamb or beef stock, preferably home-made (see page 27)

salt and pepper

Preparation and cooking time: 1¼–1¾ hours, plus overnight soaking

Each serving provides

kcal 514, protein 53 g, fat 13 g (of which saturated fat 5 g), carbohydrate 51 g (of which sugars 11 g), fibre 8 g

✓✓✓	A, B$_1$, B$_2$, B$_6$, B$_{12}$, C, E, folate, niacin, calcium, zinc
✓✓	iron, selenium

1 Drain and rinse the flageolets, then place them in a large saucepan and pour over enough cold water to come up to about twice the depth of the beans. Cover the pan with its lid and bring to the boil. Skim off any scum, then reduce the heat and add 2 of the garlic cloves and the bay leaf. Cover the pan again and cook the beans over a low heat for about 1¼ hours or until tender.

2 Meanwhile, preheat the oven to 180°C (350°F, gas mark 4). Untie the lamb if necessary, season the inside with salt and pepper and sprinkle over the leaves from half of the rosemary sprigs. Place the lemon slices down the middle, then roll up the meat and tie it with string at 2.5 cm (1 in) intervals. Rub the outside of the joint with 1 tsp of the oil and season with salt and pepper to taste. Cut the remaining garlic cloves into slivers. With the tip of a knife, cut slits in the lamb and insert the garlic slivers and the remaining rosemary, broken into little sprigs.

3 Weigh the lamb and calculate the cooking time (see page 22), then set it, rounded side up, on a rack in a shallow roasting tin. Put into the oven and roast for the calculated time.

4 About 30 minutes before the lamb is ready, cook the potatoes in boiling water for about 10 minutes or until just tender, then drain well. When the lamb is done, transfer it to a carving board, cover with foil and keep warm. Drain off any fat from the roasting tin.

5 Heat the remaining 1 tsp oil in a large saucepan over a moderate heat. Add the shallots and cook for 2 minutes, stirring occasionally, then add the tomatoes and cook for 3–4 minutes. Drain the cooked beans and discard the bay leaf. Add the beans to the shallot and tomato mixture, then add the parsley. Cover and cook for a further 3–4 minutes, then gently stir in the potatoes. Season to taste and keep warm over a low heat.

6 Put the green beans in a saucepan and barely cover with boiling water. Cook over a moderate heat for 3–4 minutes or until just tender. Drain well and keep warm.

7 To make the gravy, place the roasting tin on top of the cooker and pour in the wine and stock. Bring to the boil over a moderate heat, stirring and scraping the bottom of the tin to mix in any cooking residue, then boil for 1 minute. Keep hot over a low heat.

8 Carve the lamb. Put the bean and potato mixture on a warmed serving platter and arrange the slices of lamb on top. Serve the gravy and green beans separately.

Plus points

• Beans are an excellent source of protein and soluble fibre. Unfortunately they can produce side effects such as wind and bloating. To prevent this, cook dried beans thoroughly or rinse canned ones.

Another idea

• For a quick version, use 4 lean lamb leg steaks, 600 g (1 lb 5 oz) in total, trimmed of fat and sprinkled with salt, pepper and a little chopped fresh rosemary. Drain 2 cans flageolet or cannellini beans, about 400 g each, and put in a saucepan with 1 tsp extra virgin olive oil, 2 tbsp water, 1 grated carrot, the grated zest of ½ lemon, 2 finely chopped garlic cloves and 3 tbsp chopped parsley. Cover and cook over a low heat for 10 minutes or until hot and bubbling, stirring frequently. Meanwhile, heat 1 tsp olive oil in a non-stick frying pan over a moderately high heat, put in the lamb and fry for 2 minutes on each side for medium-rare, or 3 minutes per side for medium. Serve the lamb on top of the beans, accompanied by new potatoes and green beans.

Gingered roast pork

Roast pork with apple sauce, an all-time favourite, is given a new twist in this dish inspired by German cuisine. It is absolutely delicious served with roast or jacket baked potatoes and seasonal green vegetables.

Serves 6

900 g (2 lb) boned loin of pork without skin, trimmed of fat

3 dessert apples

1 small onion, finely chopped

75 g (2½ oz) ready-to-eat prunes, chopped

75 g (2½ oz) gingersnap biscuits, crushed

1 egg yolk

300 ml (10 fl oz) chicken stock

200 ml (7 fl oz) dry white wine

4 tbsp extra virgin olive oil

900 g (2 lb) parsnips, quartered

1 tbsp clear honey

500 g (1 lb 2 oz) shallots

salt and pepper

Apple sauce

500 g (1 lb 2 oz) cooking apples, peeled, cored and chopped

2.5 cm (1 in) piece fresh root ginger, finely chopped

2 tbsp caster sugar

Preparation time: 1¼ hours

Cooking time: 2 hours

Each serving provides

kcal 391, **protein** 8 g, **fat** 12 g (of which saturated fat 3 g), **carbohydrate** 60 g (of which sugars 43 g), **fibre** 12 g

✓✓✓	B₁, B₂, B₆, C, E, folate, niacin
✓✓	potassium
✓	B₂, calcium, iron, zinc

1. Preheat the oven to 180ºC (350ºF, gas mark 4). Place the pork, skinned side down, on a chopping board. Slit the joint lengthways, cutting two-thirds of the way through the meat, then open it out like a book.

2. Peel, core and finely chop 1 of the dessert apples, then mix with the onion, prunes, biscuits, egg yolk and seasoning to taste. Spoon onto the pork, spreading evenly, then press the joint back together. Tie into a neat shape with fine string.

3. Put the joint, skinned side up, into a roasting tin and pour in the stock and wine. Cover the tin with foil, twisting the ends tightly over the edges. Put into the oven and roast for 2 hours.

4. After 45 minutes, heat the oil in a second roasting tin on the shelf above the pork for 5 minutes. Add the parsnips and put to roast, turning them once or twice.

5. Meanwhile, make the apple sauce. Put the apples, ginger, sugar and 2 tbsp water into a small saucepan. Cover and simmer, stirring occasionally, for 10 minutes or until pulpy. Remove from the heat and set aside.

6. When the pork has been cooking for 1¼ hours, remove the foil and drizzle the meat with the honey. Add the shallots to the parsnips, toss together and continue roasting.

7. About 20 minutes before the end of the cooking time, peel, core and thickly slice the remaining 2 dessert apples, then add them to the vegetables.

8. Transfer the pork to a carving board, cover with foil and keep warm. Strain the cooking liquid into a saucepan, then skim off any fat. Boil the cooking liquid, stirring constantly, for 2 minutes. Pour into a sauceboat. Carve the pork and serve immediately, with the roasted vegetables, apple sauce and gravy.

Plus points

- Prunes supply useful amounts of iron, potassium and vitamin B₆, and they also contain fibre, which helps to prevent constipation. Prune juice contains an ingredient that has an additional laxative effect, which is why some people drink the juice rather than eat the fruit itself.

- Ginger is a useful alternative remedy for travel sickness or morning sickness. In herbal medicine it is used to aid digestion, to protect against respiratory and digestive infections, and to relieve flatulence.

Some more ideas

• Instead of fresh pork use smoked pork loin, which is slightly milder and sweeter than smoked gammon. Look for it in the cooked meats section of large supermarkets, or ask your butcher if he can get it for you.

• Spice the pork and sauce with cardamom rather than ginger. In the stuffing, substitute fresh breadcrumbs for the gingersnap biscuits and 85 g (3 oz) chopped ready-to-eat dried apricots for the diced apple and add the seeds of 4 crushed cardamom pods. In the apple sauce replace the ginger with the seeds of 6–8 crushed cardamom pods. Serve the cardamom pork with spiced roast vegetables: add 500 g (1 lb 2 oz) potatoes, peeled and cut in chunks, to the parsnips. Toss in the hot oil, then sprinkle with 1 tsp each crushed coriander and cumin seeds and turmeric.

• For an alternative accompaniment, stir-fry 500 g (1 lb 2 oz) finely shredded red cabbage in 1 tbsp sunflower oil for 5 minutes. Add 2 diced dessert apples, 3 tbsp wine vinegar, 3 tbsp water, 2 tbsp honey and salt and pepper to taste. Mix together, cover and simmer for 4–5 minutes.

• As a change from roast vegetables, serve with puréed celeriac. Cook 900 g (2 lb) diced celeriac in boiling water for 15 minutes, then mash or purée with 4 tbsp milk and seasoning.

103

Mediterranean stuffed vegetables

An array of colourful stuffed vegetables makes an appetising main dish, ideal for an informal help-yourself meal. Serve with lots of French bread and a mixed leaf salad.

Serves 4

100 g (3½ oz) long-grain rice

250 g (8½ oz) lean minced lamb

1 onion, chopped

4 peppers

4 beefsteak tomatoes, ripe but firm

2 large courgettes, about 225 g (8 oz) each

1 tbsp extra virgin olive oil

3 garlic cloves, coarsely chopped

170 g (6 oz) baby spinach leaves

2 tbsp shredded fresh basil

1 egg, lightly beaten

salt and pepper

To serve

2–3 tbsp shredded fresh basil

Preparation time: 45 minutes
Cooking time: 45–50 minutes

Each serving provides

kcal 324, protein 21 g, fat 15 g (of which saturated fat 5 g), carbohydrate 27 g (of which sugars 18 g), fibre 7 g

✓✓✓	A, B₁, B₆, B₁₂, C, E, folate, niacin, zinc
✓✓	B₂, iron, potassium
✓	calcium

1 Cook the rice in a saucepan of boiling water for 10–12 minutes, or according to the packet instructions, until tender. Drain.

2 While the rice is cooking, put the lamb and onion in a non-stick frying pan and fry until the lamb is lightly browned and cooked through and the onion has softened. Turn and break up the meat as it cooks so it browns evenly. Place a sieve over a bowl and tip the meat into it. The fat will drip through and can be discarded.

3 Cut each pepper in half lengthways through the stalk and remove the core and seed. Cut the tops (stalk end) off the tomatoes and hollow out the insides. Chop the tops and hollowed-out flesh and place in a bowl with any tomato juices. Cut the courgettes in half lengthways and hollow out the centres to leave shells 5 mm (¼ in) thick. Chop the hollowed-out courgette flesh and add it to the chopped tomatoes.

4 Preheat the oven to 180°C (350°F, gas mark 4). Heat the olive oil in a non-stick frying pan, add the garlic and chopped vegetables, and cook, stirring, until they soften slightly. Add the spinach and cook over a moderate heat for a minute or so until wilted. Remove from the heat and add the basil, rice and lamb. Add the egg, season with salt and pepper to taste and mix well.

5 Spoon the stuffing into the pepper, tomato and courgette shells. Arrange the peppers and courgettes in a single layer in 1 or 2 roasting tins. The vegetables should not be too crowded together. Cover with foil or a lid and roast for 15 minutes. Add the tomatoes and continue roasting for 15 minutes or until the vegetables are almost tender.

6 Uncover the vegetables and roast for a further 15–20 minutes or until they are tender and the tops are lightly browned. Serve either warm or cool, sprinkled with the shredded fresh basil.

Plus points

● The Mediterranean-style vegetables used in this dish are high in phytochemicals and antioxidant vitamins. Among these is beta-carotene from the peppers, spinach, tomatoes and courgettes. The antioxidant properties of beta-carotene help to protect cells from damage by free radicals produced in the body in response to stress.

● Courgettes belong to the same family as melons, pumpkins and cucumber. Their skin is rich in beta-carotene, and they also provide niacin and vitamin B₆.

Another idea

• Make Middle Eastern-style stuffed vegetables. Use brown rice instead of white rice and combine it with the fried lamb and onion. Add 3 thinly sliced spring onions, 3 chopped garlic cloves, 2 tbsp each chopped fresh dill and mint, ½ tsp ground cumin, a good pinch of ground cinnamon, 3 tbsp plain low-fat yogurt, 2 tbsp raisins, the juice of ½ lemon, and salt and pepper to taste. Cut 2 aubergines in half lengthways and steam for 5 minutes or until just tender. Leave until cool enough to handle, then hollow them out, leaving shells about 5 mm (¼ in) thick. Dice the flesh and add it to the rice and lamb mixture. Blanch 4 large Savoy cabbage leaves for 30–60 seconds or until pliable. Arrange the aubergine shells in a roasting tin and spoon in some of the filling.

Roll the rest of the filling in the cabbage leaves and place in the tin. Mix 1 can chopped tomatoes, about 225 g, and their juices with 120 ml (4 fl oz) lamb or vegetable stock and spoon around the vegetables. Cover the tin with foil. Roast for 30 minutes. Uncover and continue roasting for 15–20 minutes or until the tops of the vegetables are tinged a light brown. Serve hot or cool, garnished with chopped fresh mint.

Steak and kidney pies

A crisp filo pastry topping makes an attractive change from the more traditional lid of puff or shortcrust on these individual pies – and it's lighter and less fatty too. Serve with generous helpings of vegetables such as freshly cooked carrots and sugarsnap peas, plus more potatoes to boost the starchy carbohydrates.

Serves 4

4 tbsp extra virgin olive oil

340 g (12 oz) lean rump steak, trimmed of fat and cut into 4 cm (1½ in) pieces

2 lamb's kidneys, cored and diced

250 g (8½ oz) shallots, halved

2 garlic cloves, crushed

2 tsp fresh thyme leaves

1 bay leaf

1 tbsp Worcestershire sauce

150 ml (5 fl oz) beef stock, preferably home-made (see page 27)

150 ml (5 fl oz) stout

225 g (8 oz) button mushrooms, halved

3 carrots, cut into chunks

250 g (8½ oz) new potatoes, scrubbed and cut into 2.5 cm (1 in) dice

8 large sheets filo pastry, about 36 x 18 cm (14 x 7 in) each, thawed if frozen

salt and pepper

Preparation time: 1 hour 50 minutes
Cooking time: 20 minutes

Each serving provides

kcal 405, protein 29 g, fat 16 g (of which saturated fat 3 g), carbohydrate 35 g (of which sugars 9 g), fibre 4 g

✓✓✓ A, B₁, B₂, B₆, B₁₂, C, E, niacin, selenium, zinc

✓✓ C, folate, iron, potassium

1 Heat 2 tbsp of the oil in a large pan, add the steak and fry for 2–3 minutes, turning to brown the pieces on all sides. Remove with a draining spoon and set aside. Add the kidneys to the pan and brown for 1–2 minutes, then remove with the draining spoon.

2 Fry the shallots for 1 minute, then return the steak and kidney to the pan, together with the garlic, thyme, bay leaf, Worcestershire sauce, stock and stout. Stir well and bring to the boil. Reduce the heat, cover and simmer gently for 1 hour. Add the mushrooms, carrots and potatoes, and stir to mix. Cover again and simmer for a further 30 minutes.

3 Preheat the oven to 190°C (375°F, gas mark 5). With a draining spoon, lift out the steak and kidney mixture and divide among four 360 ml (12 fl oz) pie dishes. Discard the bay leaf. The ingredients will have produced a lot of liquid, so boil for about 5 minutes or until reduced to about 450 ml (15 fl oz). Season to taste, then pour over the meat and allow to cool slightly.

4 Lightly brush a sheet of filo with some of the remaining 2 tbsp oil. Place another sheet on top and brush lightly with more oil. Scrunch up the 2 sheets together to fit the top of a dish and lay it over the meat, then trim all around the edge with scissors. Repeat with the remaining 3 dishes. Bake the pies for 20 minutes or until the pastry is golden brown and the filling is hot.

Some more ideas

• Add a strip of pared orange zest with the garlic and herbs in step 2. Remove the orange zest at the beginning of step 3, and add 150 g (5½ oz) diced swede, 2 sliced celery sticks and 125 g (4½ oz) potatoes with the mushrooms.

• Instead of kidneys, add 1 can smoked oysters, about 85 g, drained, to the pie dishes before covering with pastry.

Plus points

• Suet or puff pastry is traditionally used for steak and kidney pies, but both of these pastries are high in saturated fat. The filo used here is very low in fat, and its light texture complements the robust flavours of the steak and kidney. Brushing it with olive oil rather than the more usual butter helps to reduce the saturated fat even further.

Lamb kebabs with fig rice

Marinating is the key to success for these tender, juicy and sweet-tasting kebabs. Just half an hour will add delicious flavours to the lamb, although overnight is better if you have time. Serve with a leafy mixed salad, and a bowl of plain low-fat yogurt mixed with grated cucumber and chopped fresh mint and flat-leaf parsley.

Serves 4

3 tbsp extra virgin olive oil

grated zest and juice of ½ lemon

1 large garlic clove, crushed

1 tbsp chopped fresh thyme

400 g (14 oz) lean lamb neck fillets, trimmed of fat and cut into 5 mm (¼ in) cubes

8 shallots

1 aubergine, about 280 g (10 oz)

2 courgettes, about 400 g (14 oz) in total

1 lemon

salt and pepper

Fig rice

300 g (10½ oz) basmati rice, well rinsed

100 g (3½ oz) dried figs, chopped

25 g (scant 1 oz) toasted flaked almonds

1 tbsp lemon juice, or to taste

Preparation time: 30 minutes, plus at least 30 minutes marinating

Cooking time: 15–20 minutes

Each serving provides

kcal 680, **protein** 29 g, **fat** 27 g (of which saturated fat 8 g), **carbohydrate** 78 g (of which sugars 18 g), **fibre** 5 g

✓✓✓	B₁, B₂, B₆, B₁₂, C, niacin, zinc
✓✓	folate, calcium, iron
✓	A

1 In a shallow dish whisk the oil with the lemon zest and juice, garlic, thyme and salt and pepper to taste. Add the cubes of lamb and coat them in the mixture, then cover the dish with cling film. Leave to marinate in a cool place for 30 minutes, or in the fridge overnight.

2 Cut each shallot in half through the root. Cut the aubergine lengthways in half, then cut each half across into 8 slices. Cut each courgette into 8 slices and the lemon into 8 wedges.

3 When ready to cook, preheat the grill to high. Remove the lamb from the marinade with a draining spoon, shaking the marinade back into the dish. Place the vegetables in the marinade and turn them to moisten.

4 Thread the lamb and vegetables onto 8 long metal kebab skewers, placing the lemon wedges on the ends. Don't pack the ingredients too tightly together on the skewers or they will not cook thoroughly. Put the skewers under the grill, about 7.5 cm (3 in) away from the heat if possible, or reduce the heat of the grill to moderate. Cook for 6–8 minutes on each side.

5 Meanwhile, put the rice in a saucepan of cold water and bring to the boil, then cover and simmer gently for 10 minutes, or according to the packet instructions, until tender. Drain well and stir in the chopped figs, flaked almonds and salt and pepper to taste. Add the lemon juice. Serve the fig rice on warmed plates, with the lamb kebabs placed on top.

Plus points

• Aubergines are satisfyingly filling but low in calories – 100 g (3½ oz) contains just 15 kcal. They are renowned for absorbing oil when fried, but cooking them this way keeps the fat content very low.

• Dried figs are a good source of potassium, calcium and iron as well as fibre, both soluble and insoluble. Insoluble fibre helps to prevent constipation and bowel disorders.

• Rice is a good gluten-free starchy carbohydrate, useful for those who suffer from coeliac disease.

Some more ideas

- Serve with quinoa instead of basmati rice. Cook 225 g (8 oz) quinoa with 4 times its volume of water for 15–20 minutes.
- Flavour the rice or quinoa with sultanas or chopped dried apricots instead of the figs.

- For Greek-style kebabs, marinate the lamb in a mixture of 200 g (7 oz) plain low-fat yogurt, the grated zest and juice of ½ lemon, 1 tbsp extra virgin olive oil, 1 crushed garlic clove and 2 tbsp chopped fresh mint. Toss the vegetables with 2 tbsp extra virgin olive oil and thread onto

skewers. Thread the lamb onto separate skewers. Grill the lamb and vegetable kebabs for 6–8 minutes on each side. Serve in warm pitta breads with shredded lettuce, diced cucumber, sliced tomatoes and a few stoned and sliced black olives.

Perfect pot roast

This long-simmered, one-pot meal is wonderfully satisfying. It can be prepared ahead, so it's perfect for family dinners as well as informal entertaining. Serve with a crunchy mixed salad and bread.

Serves 6

1 tsp extra virgin olive oil

1 kg (2¼ lb) piece boneless beef chuck, about 7.5 cm (3 in) thick, trimmed of fat and tied

2 large onions, finely chopped

1 celery stick, finely chopped

3 garlic cloves, crushed

250 ml (8½ fl oz) dry red or white wine

1 can chopped tomatoes, about 225 g

1 large carrot, grated

1 tsp chopped fresh thyme

450 ml (15 fl oz) beef stock, preferably home-made (see page 27)

600 g (1 lb 5 oz) new potatoes, scrubbed and quartered

340 g (12 oz) celeriac, cut into 2.5 cm (1 in) cubes

340 g (12 oz) swede, cut into 2.5 cm (1 in) cubes

4 carrots, about 280 g (10 oz) in total, sliced

salt and pepper

3 tbsp chopped parsley to garnish

Preparation and cooking time: 4 hours

Each serving provides

kcal 399, **protein** 43 g, **fat** 12 g (of which saturated fat 4 g), **carbohydrate** 33 g (of which sugars 15 g), **fibre** 8 g

✓✓✓	A, B₁, B₆, B₁₂, C, folate, niacin, zinc
✓✓	B₂, iron
✓	selenium

1 Preheat the oven to 160°C (325°F, gas mark 3). Heat the oil in a large flameproof casserole. Add the beef and brown it over a moderately high heat for 6–8 minutes or until it is well coloured on all sides. Remove the meat to a plate.

2 Reduce the heat to moderate. Add the onions, celery and garlic and cook, stirring frequently, for about 3 minutes or until the onions begin to soften. Add the wine and let it bubble for about 1 minute, then add the tomatoes with their juice and the grated carrot. Cook for a further 2 minutes.

3 Return the beef to the casserole together with any juices that have collected on the plate and the chopped thyme. Tuck a piece of greaseproof paper or foil around the top of the meat, turning back the corners so that it doesn't touch the liquid, then cover with a tight-fitting lid. Transfer the casserole to the oven and cook for 2½ hours.

4 About 20 minutes before the end of the cooking time, bring the stock to the boil in a deep saucepan with a lid. Add the potatoes, celeriac, swede and sliced carrots. Cover and simmer gently for 12–15 minutes or until they are starting to become tender.

5 Meanwhile, remove the beef from the casserole and set aside. Remove any fat from the cooking liquid, either by spooning it off or by using a bulb baster, then purée the casseroled vegetables and liquid in a blender or food processor until smooth. Season to taste.

6 Drain the potatoes and other root vegetables, reserving the liquid. Make a layer of the vegetables in the casserole, put the beef on top and add the remaining root vegetables and their cooking liquid. Pour over the puréed sauce. Cover the casserole and return to the oven to cook for 20 minutes or until the root vegetables are tender.

7 Remove the beef to a carving board, cover and leave to rest for 10 minutes. Keep the vegetables and sauce in the oven turned down to low.

8 Carve the beef and arrange on warmed plates with the vegetables and sauce. Sprinkle with the parsley and serve immediately.

Plus points

• Swede is a member of the cruciferous family of vegetables. It is a useful source of vitamin C and beta-carotene and rich in phytochemicals that are believed to help protect against cancer.

• A freshly dug potato may contain as much as ten times more vitamin C than one that has been stored.

Some more ideas

- Brisket can be used instead of chuck, as can topside of beef.
- Any leftover beef can be chopped or shredded and mixed with the sauce and/or a freshly made tomato sauce, then served over spaghetti or other pasta.
- Substitute a boneless gammon joint, soaked if necessary, for the beef. Soften 1 chopped onion in 1 tsp extra virgin olive oil with 2 chopped garlic cloves (omit the celery). Add the wine (use white) and gammon (there is no need to brown it first). Omit the tomatoes, grated carrot and thyme and add 750 ml (1¼ pints) unsalted vegetable stock, 3 cloves, 1½ tsp mustard powder and 1 strip of orange zest. Cover and simmer for 1¼ hours, adding the root vegetables after 25 minutes. When the meat is cooked, transfer it to a carving board as in step 7. Strain the cooking liquid and remove the fat, then boil rapidly until reduced to 600 ml (1 pint). Stir in 2 tbsp cornflour mixed with 1½ tbsp cold water and boil until the liquid has thickened. Finish as in the main recipe.

Lamb, butternut and barley stew

Like Irish stew and Lancashire hotpot, this hearty dish is made with good-quality lamb, plus lots of vegetables, pearl barley, and bay leaves and thyme for flavouring. It is simple to make, and comes out of the oven smelling and tasting absolutely wonderful. Serve with purple sprouting broccoli or curly kale and baked potatoes.

Serves 4

1 tbsp extra virgin olive oil

4 lamb chops, about 450 g (1 lb) in total, trimmed of fat

2 onions, quartered lengthways

2 large leeks, about 400 g (14 oz) in total, cut into 2.5 cm (1 in) pieces

1 butternut squash, about 600 g (1 lb 5 oz), peeled, seeded and cut into 2.5 cm (1 in) chunks

2 turnips, about 200 g (7 oz) in total, quartered lengthways

100 g (3½ oz) pearl barley

900 ml (1½ pints) hot lamb stock, preferably home-made (see page 27)

2 bay leaves

2 large sprigs of fresh thyme

salt and pepper

2 tbsp chopped parsley to garnish

Preparation time: 20 minutes, plus 10 minutes standing

Cooking time: about 1½ hours

Each serving provides

kcal 418, protein 30 g, fat 15 g (of which saturated fat 6 g), carbohydrate 45 g (of which sugars 16 g), fibre 7 g

✓✓✓	A, B$_1$, B$_6$, B$_{12}$, C, E, folate, niacin, zinc
✓✓	iron, magnesium, potassium
✓	B$_2$, calcium

---

1 Preheat the oven to 160ºC (325ºF, gas mark 3). Heat the oil in a large flameproof casserole, add the chops and brown them on both sides. Remove the chops and set aside.

2 Add the onion wedges and fry for about 5 minutes or until browned on all sides. Stir in the leeks, squash and turnips. Cover and sweat gently for 5 minutes.

3 Sprinkle in the pearl barley and cook, stirring, for 1 minute, then pour in the hot stock. Tuck the chops in with the vegetables, and add the bay leaves, thyme and seasoning to taste. Bring to the boil, then cover the casserole. Transfer to the oven and cook for 1¼ hours or until the meat and vegetables are very tender.

4 Remove the casserole from the oven and let stand for 10 minutes, to allow the barley to soak up more of the stock. Taste the stew for seasoning and serve hot, sprinkled with parsley.

Some more ideas

• For extra piquancy, add a few dashes of Worcestershire sauce or a couple of crushed garlic cloves with the herbs in step 3.

• Try diced carrots, swede or potatoes instead of the butternut squash and turnips.

• Make the stew into a hearty soup. Brown 340 g (12 oz) trimmed and diced boneless lean leg of lamb in the oil. Remove from the pan. Add 2 chopped onions, 2 chopped leeks, 400 g (14 oz) diced swede and 200 g (7 oz) diced carrot. Sweat for 5 minutes, then stir in the pearl barley, 1.3 litres (2¼ pints) hot lamb or vegetable stock, 2 bay leaves and 1 tbsp chopped fresh thyme or 2 tbsp chopped parsley. Season, then cook in the oven for 1¼ hours or until the meat and vegetables are very tender.

Plus points

• Pearl barley is low in fat and rich in starchy carbohydrate, and according to folklore it is a good food for potency and vigour. Roman gladiators ate barley to build up their strength, similar to the way today's athletes eat pasta the night before they compete.

• Butternut squash is an excellent source of beta-carotene, which converts to vitamin A in the body. This vitamin is essential for good night vision. Butternut squash is also a good source of vitamin C and a useful source of vitamin E. All of these vitamins act as antioxidants, fighting against some cancers and preventing heart disease.

New England simmered beef

This traditional American dish is a one-pot meal of succulent beef and tender-crisp vegetables in a nutritious and tasty broth. The tangy beetroot and onion relish cuts through the richness of the meat and is an inspired finishing touch. Serve with crusty bread to mop up the juices.

Serves 4

675 g (1½ lb) piece lean chuck steak, trimmed of fat

3 sprigs of fresh thyme

3 sprigs of parsley

1 large bay leaf

2 large garlic cloves, sliced

10 black peppercorns, lightly crushed

250 g (8½ oz) leek, sliced

1 celery stick, cut into 7.5 cm (3 in) pieces

300 g (10½ oz) baby new potatoes, scrubbed

12 small shallots

300 g (10½ oz) baby turnips

300 g (10½ oz) baby carrots

150 g (5½ oz) Savoy cabbage, cored and finely shredded

salt and pepper

finely chopped parsley to garnish

Beetroot and onion relish

340 g (12 oz) cooked beetroot, peeled and finely diced

6 spring onions, finely chopped

3 tbsp finely chopped parsley

Preparation time: 25 minutes

Cooking time: about 2½ hours

1 Place the beef in a flameproof casserole. Add about 1.5 litres (2¾ pints) water to cover the meat very generously. Bring to the boil over a high heat, skimming the surface as necessary to remove all the grey foam.

2 As soon as the liquid comes to the boil, reduce the heat to very low. Tie the thyme, parsley, bay leaf, garlic and peppercorns in a little muslin bag and add to the pan with the leek and celery. Half-cover the pan and simmer gently, skimming the surface when necessary, for 1¾–2 hours or until the beef is very tender when pierced with the tip of a sharp knife.

3 Meanwhile, make the beetroot relish. Place the beetroot in a bowl with the spring onions and parsley. Season with salt and pepper to taste and gently stir together. Cover and chill.

4 Preheat the oven on a low setting. When the meat is tender, use 2 large spoons to transfer it to an ovenproof dish. Spoon over enough of the cooking liquid to cover the meat, then tightly cover the dish with foil. Place in the oven to keep warm.

5 Remove the muslin bag from the casserole and discard. Add the potatoes and shallots to the casserole with ½ tsp salt, increase the heat and cook for 5 minutes. Add the turnips and

carrots and simmer for a further 15 minutes or until the vegetables are tender. With a draining spoon transfer them to the dish with the meat.

6 Add the cabbage to the broth in the casserole and simmer for about 3 minutes or until it is tender. Remove with a draining spoon and add to the other vegetables.

7 To serve, slice the beef against the grain and place the slices in soup plates or plates with rims. Top with a selection of vegetables and spoon over some of the broth. Sprinkle with parsley and serve with the relish.

Plus points

- Traditionally, beetroot was believed to be good for the health of the blood – probably because of its deep red colour. It does contain folate, an essential vitamin for healthy cells and the prevention of anaemia, and is also believed to contain anti-carcinogens.

Another idea

• This is traditionally made using mainly root vegetables, but it is also delicious made with green vegetables. Pod 500 g (1 lb 2 oz) fresh peas (or use 250 g/8½ oz frozen peas); trim 250 g (8½ oz) young asparagus tips; and cut 250 g (8½ oz) tender, thin leeks across into 5 cm (2 in) slices. In step 5, strain the broth, and discard the muslin bag, leek and celery.

Add the asparagus to the casserole and simmer for 3 minutes, then add the peas and thin leeks and simmer for another 3 minutes or until all the vegetables are tender. Stir in 250 g (8½ oz) baby leaf spinach and leave the casserole on the heat for a further 1–2 minutes, just until the spinach leaves wilt. Sprinkle with very finely sliced spring onions and serve with boiled tiny new potatoes in their skins.

Each serving provides

kcal 391, **protein** 45 g, **fat** 8 g (of which saturated fat 3 g), **carbohydrate** 36 g (of which sugars 23 g), **fibre** 10 g

✓✓✓	A, B₁, B₂, B₆, B₁₂, C, E, niacin, zinc
✓✓	iron, selenium
✓	calcium

Normandy pork with apples, celery and walnuts

Fresh and fruity, this casserole comes from northwestern France, where cider apples grow in profusion. A dish of rice is cooked in the oven at the same time, making this a very simple meal to prepare. Serve with generous helpings of green vegetables, such as French beans or mange-tout.

Serves 4

2 tbsp sunflower oil

500 g (1 lb 2 oz) pork fillet (tenderloin), trimmed of fat and cut into cubes

8 celery sticks, cut across into 5 cm (2 in) lengths, leaves reserved and chopped

1 onion, roughly chopped

450 ml (15 fl oz) cider or apple juice

1 bay leaf

300 g (10½ oz) long-grain rice

900 ml (1½ pints) boiling chicken stock

3 crisp dessert apples, preferably red-skinned

100 g (3½ oz) broken walnuts

salt and pepper

Preparation time: 15 minutes
Cooking time: about 2 hours

Each serving provides

kcal 734, **protein** 37 g, **fat** 27 g (of which saturated fat 3 g), **carbohydrate** 91 g (of which sugars 17 g), **fibre** 4 g

✓✓✓	B₁, B₆, B₁₂, niacin, copper, zinc
✓✓	B₂, C, potassium
✓	iron

1 Preheat the oven to 160°C (325°F, gas mark 3). Heat the oil in a flameproof casserole, add the pork and fry, stirring frequently, for 5 minutes or until browned on all sides. Add the celery and onion and fry gently for about 10 minutes or until softened.

2 Pour in the cider or apple juice and add the bay leaf. Season with salt and pepper to taste. Bring to the boil, then cover the casserole and transfer to the oven. Cook for 1¼ hours or until the pork is tender.

3 About 40 minutes before the pork is ready, put the rice in an ovenproof dish and pour over the boiling stock. Stir well, then cover and put into the oven to cook with the pork.

4 About 25 minutes before the end of the cooking time, quarter and core the apples but do not peel them. Slice the quarters thickly, then add to the pork and continue cooking.

5 Meanwhile, heat a small frying pan over a moderate heat, add the walnuts and cook, stirring, until lightly toasted. When the pork is tender, stir in the walnuts and taste for seasoning. Garnish with the chopped celery leaves and serve hot, with the rice.

Some more ideas

● Replace the pork with cubes of lean chuck steak and increase the cooking time in the oven to about 2 hours.

● Add 1 chopped garlic clove and 1 tsp chopped fresh root ginger to the onion and use orange juice instead of the cider or apple juice. Replace the apple slices with the segments of 2 oranges, adding them 10 minutes before the end of the cooking time. Garnish the casserole with shreds of orange zest. Cook the rice in a mixture of orange juice and vegetable stock.

Plus points

● Some studies indicate that a small quantity of walnuts eaten regularly can help to reduce high blood cholesterol levels. Walnuts may also guard against cardiovascular disease and cancer because of the antioxidants they contain – selenium, zinc, copper and vitamin E.

● Apples and apple juice provide good amounts of potassium. Along with sodium, potassium is an important mineral for maintaining fluid balance, regulating blood pressure and keeping a healthy heart.

Goulash soup

This rich meal-in-a-bowl combines beef with vegetables and dumplings and the three essential ingredients of an authentic goulash – paprika, onions and caraway seeds. Serve with boiled or steamed potatoes.

Serves 4

1½ tbsp sunflower oil

2 large onions, sliced

2 garlic cloves, finely chopped

500 g (1 lb 2 oz) lean chuck steak, trimmed of fat and cut into 2 cm (¾ in) cubes

2 large carrots, diced

1 tbsp paprika

¼ tsp caraway seeds

1 can chopped tomatoes, about 400 g

750 ml (1¼ pints) beef stock, preferably home-made (see page 27)

170 g (6 oz) white cabbage, finely shredded

salt and pepper

chopped parsley to garnish

Parsley and onion dumplings

1 tbsp sunflower oil

1 onion, finely chopped

1 egg

3 tbsp semi-skimmed milk

3 tbsp chopped parsley

120 g (4¼ oz) fresh white breadcrumbs

Preparation time: 30 minutes

Cooking time: 1½ hours

Each serving provides

kcal 479, **protein** 38 g, **fat** 18 g (of which saturated fat 5 g), **carbohydrate** 46 g (of which sugars 19 g), **fibre** 6 g

✓✓✓ A, B₁, B₆, B₁₂, C, E, folate, niacin, zinc

✓✓ B₂, iron, selenium

---

1 Heat the oil in a large saucepan, add the onions and garlic and cook over a moderately low heat, stirring frequently, for 10 minutes or until beginning to brown.

2 Add the cubes of beef and cook, stirring, for 5 minutes or until browned all over. Add the carrots, paprika, caraway seeds, tomatoes with their juice and stock. Season with salt and pepper to taste. Stir well and bring to the boil, then cover and simmer gently for 1 hour or until the beef is just tender.

3 Meanwhile, make the dumplings. Heat the oil in a frying pan, add the onion and cook over a low heat, stirring frequently, for about 10 minutes or until softened but not coloured. In a bowl, beat the egg and milk together, then add the onion, parsley and breadcrumbs. Season with salt and pepper to taste and mix well.

4 Add the cabbage to the saucepan and stir to mix with the beef and other vegetables. With wet hands, shape the dumpling mixture into 12 walnut-sized balls. Add to the pan, cover and cook for a further 15 minutes or until the dumplings are cooked. Taste for seasoning and serve hot in warmed deep soup plates, sprinkled with chopped parsley.

Plus points

- Cabbage belongs to the brassica group of cruciferous vegetables. These contain glucosinolates and other sulphur compounds associated with lowering the risk of cancer. These vegetables are also good sources of vitamin C and among the richest vegetable sources of folate.

- Dumplings are a nutritious addition to soups or stews, being filling and providing valuable starchy carbohydrate.

Some more ideas

- Replace the beef with 340 g (12 oz) stewing veal and add 100 g (3½ oz) diced smoked pork sausage with the cabbage.

- Use 1 seeded and thinly sliced red pepper instead of the cabbage.

- For a spicy soup, add 1 seeded and finely chopped fresh red chilli with the paprika.

Venison and chestnut casserole

Full of flavour but low in saturated fat, venison makes a wonderful alternative to beef for a casserole. Here port and beetroot enhance the richness, colour and flavour of the meat, and chestnuts add texture and body. For a delicious meal, serve with mashed or jacket baked potatoes or noodles.

Serves 4

25 g (scant 1 oz) butter

2 tbsp extra virgin olive oil

450 g (1 lb) boneless venison haunch or shoulder, cut into 4 cm (1½ in) cubes

2 onions, about 300 g (10½ oz) in total, sliced

2 garlic cloves, crushed

2 cooked beetroot, about 125 g (4½ oz) in total, each cut into 6 wedges

grated zest and juice of ½ large orange

100 ml (3½ fl oz) port

300 ml (10 fl oz) beef stock, preferably home-made (see page 27)

100 g (3½ oz) vacuum-packed peeled whole chestnuts

3 carrots, halved lengthways and cut into 2.5 cm (1 in) chunks

5 cm (2 in) piece fresh root ginger, grated

4 shallots, unpeeled but roots sliced off

1 tbsp plain flour

salt and pepper

Preparation time: 20 minutes

Cooking time: about 1¾ hours

Each serving provides

kcal 400, **protein** 29 g, **fat** 14 g (of which saturated fat 5 g), **carbohydrate** 35 g (of which sugars 21 g), **fibre** 5 g

✓✓✓ A, B₁, B₆, B₁₂, C, E, folate, niacin, iron, zinc

✓✓ B₂, calcium, magnesium, selenium

1 Preheat the oven to 180°C (350°F, gas mark 4). Heat 15 g (½ oz) of the butter with 1 tbsp of the oil in a large flameproof casserole. Add the venison in one layer and let it brown on each side for about 5 minutes, turning once. Do this in 2 batches if necessary. Using a draining spoon, remove the meat from the pan and set it aside on a plate.

2 Add the sliced onions to the pan and stir well. Cook over a low heat, stirring occasionally, for about 10 minutes or until the onions are softened and just beginning to turn brown.

3 Add the garlic, beetroot, and orange zest and juice. Stir well, then return the venison and its juices to the pan and pour in the port and beef stock. Bring to a simmer. Cover the casserole and transfer to the oven. Cook for 1¼ hours or until the venison is tender, adding the whole chestnuts for the last 15 minutes of cooking.

4 Meanwhile, put the carrots, ginger and shallots in a roasting tin, add the remaining 1 tbsp oil and stir until the vegetables are evenly coated. Place in the oven above the casserole and roast for 1 hour, turning the vegetables over halfway through the cooking time.

5 Blend the remaining butter with the flour to make a paste (beurre manié). Put the casserole on top of the stove over a moderately high heat and add the paste a little at a time, whisking constantly and simmering until the gravy thickens. Season to taste. Serve the venison casserole hot, with the roasted vegetables.

Plus points

• Venison is an excellent source of low-fat protein, being considerably leaner than beef. It is rich in B vitamins and iron – it contains twice as much of this mineral as beef – and a good source of phosphorus and potassium.

• Chestnuts are a low-fat, starchy nut. They are a good source of vitamin B₁ and potassium and a valuable source of fibre. They also provide small amounts of calcium, iron and vitamin B₂.

weekend meals

120

Some more ideas

• Instead of the beetroot and orange zest and juice, stir in 3 tbsp redcurrant jelly and 1 tbsp raspberry vinegar after the casserole has been cooking in the oven for 40 minutes.

• Substitute red wine for the port and add a good dash or two of balsamic vinegar instead of the orange zest and juice.

• Alcohol gives colour and richness as well as flavour to the casserole, but it can be left out – just add more stock.

• Instead of chestnuts use 100 g (3½ oz) sliced chestnut mushrooms, adding them in step 2 after the onions have cooked for 5 minutes.

• Cook the carrots and shallots in the casserole rather than separately, and add a little more stock. Omit the ginger because its flavour would upset the balance of the other ingredients.

Beef in beer

Topped with thick slices of garlic and herb bread, this classic Flemish casserole is hearty and satisfying. It's an ideal dish for entertaining because it can be prepared ahead and the quantities can be increased to feed as many as you want. Serve with mashed potatoes with chopped watercress added, and steamed seasonal greens.

Serves 4

2 tbsp extra virgin olive oil

450 g (1 lb) lean braising steak, trimmed of fat and cut into 5 cm (2 in) cubes

1 large onion, cut into wedges

2 large carrots, about 340 g (12 oz) in total, thickly sliced on the diagonal

1 large parsnip, about 170 g (6 oz), cut into cubes

1 large garlic clove, crushed

300 ml (10 fl oz) stout

300 ml (10 fl oz) beef stock, preferably home-made (see page 27)

1 tsp dried mixed herbs

1 tbsp red wine vinegar

1 tbsp wholegrain mustard

1 tsp dark soft brown sugar

salt and pepper

Garlic and herb bread topping

a piece of *campagne longue* (traditional long French loaf), weighing about 225 g (8 oz)

1 large garlic clove, crushed

1 tbsp chopped parsley

1 tbsp chopped fresh thyme

3 tbsp extra virgin olive oil

Preparation time: 15 minutes
Cooking time: 2¾ hours

1 Preheat the oven to 180°C (350°F, gas mark 4). Heat 1 tbsp of the oil in a flameproof casserole, add the beef and cook over a moderately high heat for 4–5 minutes or until browned all over. Transfer the meat and its juices to a plate.

2 Add the remaining 1 tbsp oil to the pan and reduce the heat to low, then add the onion, carrots, parsnip and garlic. Cook, stirring frequently, for 5 minutes. Return the beef and its juices to the pan together with the stout, stock, mixed herbs, vinegar, mustard and sugar. Stir well and bring to the boil. Cover the casserole and transfer to the oven. Cook for 2 hours or until the beef is tender.

3 Meanwhile, cut the piece of bread into 8 thick slices. Mix together the garlic, parsley, thyme and oil and spoon evenly over one side of each slice of bread.

4 Uncover the casserole and add salt and pepper to taste. Lay the slices of bread, oiled side up, in a circle around the top edge of the beef casserole, overlapping them slightly. Return the casserole to the oven to cook for 20–30 minutes or until the bread is golden and crisp. Serve hot.

Another idea

● For beef in red wine, use 12 whole shallots or baby onions in place of the onion, carrots and parsnips, and a full-bodied red wine instead of the stout. Omit the vinegar, mustard and sugar and add 1 tbsp redcurrant jelly instead. At the end of step 2, stir in 225 g (8 oz) sliced mushrooms and 200 g (7 oz) vacuum-packed peeled chestnuts for the last 10 minutes of the cooking time. Serve with rice and stir-fried shredded Brussels sprouts.

Plus points

● A casserole such as this makes a particularly healthy meal. Water-soluble vitamins – C and B complex – and minerals that seep from the food during the cooking process are usually thrown away with the cooking water. In casseroles, more of the nutrients are retained in the gravy.

Each serving provides

kcal 560, **protein** 35 g, **fat** 23 g (of which saturated fat 5 g), **carbohydrate** 52 g (of which sugars 17 g), **fibre** 6 g

✓✓✓	A, B₁, B₆, B₁₂, E, folate, niacin, zinc
✓✓	B₂, C, iron
✓	calcium

weekend meals

Special Meat

When entertaining family and friends

Tempting meat dishes from around the world can be impressive without being difficult or time-consuming, and they can be healthy too. Try Indonesian nasi goreng or Thai beef noodle soup, both perfect examples of low-fat dishes packed with flavour. Or cook rabbit with saffron and chickpeas Spanish-style to make a hearty one-pot meal. Combine lamb with lentils for an Indian dhansak, or with couscous to make a pretty Persian pilaf. Come nearer to home for Italian pasta with lamb, or veal escalopes with spinach and herbs from France. For a special lunch, marinate venison and pork in spices and port to make a fabulous cut-and-come-again terrine.

Pepper steak with leek mash

Potatoes – as chips, jacket baked or mashed – are a popular partner for steak. Here a mash with leeks and mustard accompanies pepper-coated fillet steaks cooked quickly on a cast-iron grill pan or griddle. Serve with a fresh, seasonal green vegetable such as French beans or broccoli.

Serves 4

2 tbsp mixed or black peppercorns, coarsely crushed

4 fillet steaks, 2.5 cm (1 in) thick, about 140 g (5 oz) each, trimmed of fat

1 tsp extra virgin olive oil

chopped parsley or snipped fresh chives to garnish

Leek and mustard mash

900 g (2 lb) floury potatoes, peeled and cut into chunks

2 tsp extra virgin olive oil

200 g (7 oz) young leeks, finely shredded

120 ml (4 fl oz) semi-skimmed milk

1 tbsp wholegrain mustard

25 g (scant 1 oz) butter

salt and pepper

Preparation and cooking time: about 1 hour

Each serving provides

kcal 465, **protein** 37 g, **fat** 18 g (of which saturated fat 8 g), **carbohydrate** 42 g (of which sugars 4 g), **fibre** 4 g

✓✓✓	B_1, B_6, B_{12}, C, E, folate, niacin
✓✓	B_2, iron, magnesium, potassium
✓	A, calcium

1 First cook the potatoes for the mash. Place the potatoes in a saucepan and pour over boiling water to cover by 5 cm (2 in). Bring back to the boil, then reduce the heat and cook for 15–20 minutes or until the potatoes are very tender.

2 Meanwhile, spread out the crushed peppercorns on a plate and press the steaks into them until they are coated with peppercorns on all sides. Set aside.

3 Heat the oil for the mash in a non-stick frying pan. Add the leeks and cook, stirring constantly, for 3–5 minutes or until tender. Transfer to a plate lined with a double thickness of kitchen paper to drain. Heat the milk in a small saucepan until hot.

4 When the potatoes are tender, drain them, shaking the colander or sieve to remove any excess water, and return them to the pan. Pour the hot milk over the potatoes, then mash them until they are completely smooth. Add the leeks, mustard and butter, and season with salt and pepper to taste. Beat well to mix, then cover and keep warm.

5 Heat a ridged cast-iron grill pan over a high heat until hot. Brush the pan with the oil, then reduce the heat to moderately high. Place the steaks in the pan and cook for 3 minutes on each side for rare; 3½ minutes on each side for medium-rare; 4 minutes on each side for medium; or 5 minutes on each side for well-done.

6 Spoon a mound of mash on each warmed plate and place a steak next to it. Drizzle any pan juices over the steaks and sprinkle with parsley or chives. Serve immediately.

Another idea

● Veal loin chops can be cooked in the same way. Use 4 chops, 2 cm (¾ in) thick and about 250 g (8½ oz) each. This weight includes the bone; it should give about 140 g (5 oz) meat. Brush the chops with oil and season with salt and pepper to taste, omitting the peppercorns. Cook as for the steaks, allowing 3 minutes on each side for medium-rare; 3½ minutes on each side for medium; or 4½ minutes on each side for well-done.

Plus points

● Adding leeks to mashed potatoes not only boosts their flavour but also adds vitamins B_1, B_6 and folate. If you include the green part of the leeks this will also provide vitamin A. Eaten regularly, leeks are believed to help reduce the risk of heart disease and stroke.

special meat

Calf's liver with rigatoni, broccoli and orange

Here's a pasta recipe which proves that the simplest ideas are the best. Savour the delicate flavour of calf's liver and broccoli with a subtle hint of garlic and chilli and the sweet freshness of orange.

Serves 4

300 g (10½ oz) calf's liver, trimmed

2 large oranges

400 g (14 oz) rigatoni, penne or other pasta shapes

250 g (8½ oz) broccoli, cut into 2.5 cm (1 in) pieces

2 tbsp extra virgin olive oil

1 garlic clove, crushed

1 small fresh red chilli, seeded and finely chopped

4 tbsp Marsala or medium sherry

1 tsp balsamic vinegar

2 tsp butter

salt and pepper

1 tsp crushed roasted coriander seeds to garnish (optional)

Preparation and cooking time: 40 minutes

Each serving provides

kcal 546, **protein** 30 g, **fat** 13 g (of which saturated fat 3 g), **carbohydrate** 84 g (of which sugars 10 g), **fibre** 6 g

✓✓✓	A, B$_1$, B$_2$, B$_6$, B$_{12}$, E, folate, niacin, iron, selenium, zinc
✓✓	magnesium
✓	calcium, potassium

1 Cut the liver into strips about 1 cm (½ in) wide and 5–6 cm (2–2½ in) long. Use a citrus zester to take the zest off one of the oranges in short strips; set the strips aside. Peel and segment both oranges, working over a bowl to catch the juice. Squeeze the juice from the peel too. Set aside 12 of the best segments, then squeeze the rest of the segments into the juice bowl to get about 5 tbsp juice in total.

2 Drop the pasta into a large saucepan of boiling water. When the water returns to the boil, cook for 10 minutes, then add the broccoli and cook for a further 2–3 minutes or until the pasta and broccoli are just tender.

3 While the broccoli and pasta are cooking, heat 1 tbsp of the oil in a frying pan large enough to take the liver in one layer. Sprinkle in the garlic and chilli and stir over a moderately high heat for 1 minute. Add the liver and toss for 1 minute or until browned. Add the Marsala or sherry and the orange zest and juice and cook for 1 more minute.

4 Drain the pasta and broccoli and return to the saucepan off the heat. Remove the liver from the sauce and add to the pasta and broccoli together with the remaining 1 tbsp oil and salt and pepper to taste. Toss well.

5 Bring the sauce to the boil and boil to reduce by half. Stir in the vinegar and butter to make the sauce glossy. Add the orange segments and warm through for 30 seconds, then spoon over the liver, pasta and broccoli and toss gently to combine. Sprinkle with the coriander seeds, if using, and serve immediately.

Plus points

• Oranges are justly famous for their vitamin C content (54 mg per 100 g/3½ oz). Vitamin C is one of the 'water-soluble' vitamins which cannot be stored by the body, so it is essential that fruit and vegetables containing vitamin C are eaten every day. As scientists have increasingly recognised, this vitamin helps to prevent a number of degenerative diseases such as heart disease and cancer, through its powerful antioxidant activity.

• Some studies have shown that chillies can help to reduce blood cholesterol levels. There are also reports suggesting that chillies can help to protect against gastric ulcers by protecting the stomach lining from irritants such as alcohol and aspirin.

special meat

Some more ideas

● If you don't want to use Marsala or sherry, add chicken stock or pasta cooking water.

● Lamb's liver can be used instead of calf's liver. It is cheaper, but just as nutritious.

● For chicken livers with rigatoni and leeks, use 300 g (10½ oz) chicken livers, cut into even-sized pieces about 2.5 cm (1 in) or larger. Heat 1 tbsp extra virgin olive oil in a large, deep frying pan, add 1 thinly sliced onion and soften for 3 minutes. Add 100 g (3½ oz) chopped chestnut mushrooms and cook for 2 minutes, then stir in 1 can chopped tomatoes, about 225 g, with the juice and add a pinch of sugar. Season with salt and pepper to taste, cover and simmer for 10 minutes. Meanwhile, cook the pasta, adding 400 g (14 oz) thinly sliced leeks for the last 3–4 minutes. Heat 2 tsp extra virgin olive oil with 15 g (½ oz) butter in a large frying pan. When it foams, add the chicken livers in a single layer and sprinkle with 2 tsp fresh thyme leaves. Leave them to brown, without stirring, for 2 minutes. Turn the livers over and cook for another 2 minutes, then season to taste. Drain the pasta and leeks, place in a shallow serving dish and spoon the tomato sauce and chicken livers on top.

Venison steaks with pears

Venison has a deep, rich flavour, and steaks taken from the loin are very tender. Here they are cooked with pears and cranberries. A root vegetable rösti is the most delicious accompaniment.

Serves 4

4 venison steaks, about 140 g (5 oz) each

coarsely ground black pepper

1 tbsp extra virgin olive oil

2 shallots, finely chopped

1 garlic clove, crushed

3 tbsp port

120 ml (4 fl oz) beef stock, preferably home-made (see page 27)

200 g (7 oz) fresh or frozen cranberries

2 ripe but firm medium-sized pears, such as Conference or Comice

1 tbsp light muscovado sugar, or to taste

Rösti

1 small celeriac, about 350 g (11½ oz)

2 medium-sized sweet potatoes, about 400 g (14 oz) in total

2 potatoes, about 400 g (14 oz) in total

1 small swede, about 400 g (14 oz)

40 g (1½ oz) unsalted butter

salt and pepper

Preparation and cooking time: about 1¼ hours

Each serving provides

kcal 515, **protein** 37 g, **fat** 14 g (of which saturated fat 7 g), **carbohydrate** 58 g (of which sugars 25 g), **fibre** 12 g

✓✓✓ A, B₁, B₆, B₁₂, C, E, folate, iron, zinc

✓✓ B₂, selenium

1 First make the rösti. Preheat the oven to 200°C (400°F, gas mark 6). Peel the celeriac, sweet potatoes, potatoes and swede and coarsely grate them, then squeeze out excess liquid. Place them in a large bowl, season with salt and pepper to taste and mix well.

2 Put half of the butter into a large ovenproof frying pan, or a round or oval baking dish or tin about 25 cm (10 in) across. Heat in the oven for 3–4 minutes or until the butter is foaming, then remove and add the grated vegetables. Press them down to make an even, compact cake. Dot with the remaining butter, then cover with foil. Bake for 15 minutes. Remove the foil and bake for 20–25 more minutes or until the top is lightly browned.

3 While the rösti is in the oven, pat the steaks dry, then season with coarsely ground black pepper. Heat the oil in a non-stick frying pan, add the steaks and fry over a moderately high heat for 3–4 minutes on each side. They will still be slightly rare in the centre. Lift out and keep warm.

4 Add the shallots and garlic to the pan and fry, stirring, for 1 minute. Add the port and boil, stirring well to deglaze the pan. Stir in the stock and cranberries and cook over a moderate heat for about 5 minutes or until the berries split and soften.

5 Meanwhile, peel and quarter the pears and remove the cores. Add to the pan and heat gently for 2–3 minutes. Add the sugar and season to taste.

6 Tip any meat juices that have collected around the steaks into the sauce and stir gently to mix. Turn out the rösti and cut it into wedges like a cake. Serve the rösti, steaks and pears on warmed individual plates, with the sauce spooned over and around.

Plus points

• Sweet potatoes are an excellent source of beta-carotene. They also provide good amounts of vitamin C and potassium, and contain more vitamin E than any other vegetable.

• Cranberries are rich in vitamin C, which boosts the immune system, and they are renowned for helping to control urinary tract infections such as cystitis. Research suggests that they can help to protect against infections of the kidney and prostate as well as preventing kidney stones.

special meat

Another idea

• Use lean boneless lamb leg steaks instead of the venison steaks and cook them in the same way. Redcurrants are the traditional accompaniment for lamb, so replace the cranberries with 200 g (7 oz) fresh or frozen redcurrants. Use red wine rather than port and lamb stock instead of beef stock. In step 5 add 1 tsp finely chopped fresh rosemary and 1 tsp redcurrant jelly to the sauce with the seasoning (omit the sugar). Stir until thoroughly combined and the jelly has melted.

Pork nasi goreng

In this Indonesian-style recipe, rice is combined with stir-fried pork, vegetables, prawns and strips of omelette to make an excellent all-in-one supper dish. Serve with a green salad tossed in a dressing spiked with fresh ginger.

Serves 6

1.2 litres (2 pints) chicken stock
450 g (1 lb) long-grain rice
2 tbsp sunflower oil
1 onion, finely chopped
2 garlic cloves, crushed
3 carrots, finely diced
2 lean boneless pork leg steaks, about 340 g
  (12 oz) in total, trimmed of fat and diced
150 g (5½ oz) button mushrooms, sliced
1 tsp mild chilli powder
½ tsp turmeric
150 g (5½ oz) frozen peas
3 tbsp tomato ketchup
2 tbsp light soy sauce
4 spring onions, thinly sliced or shredded
100 g (3½ oz) peeled cooked prawns
Omelette
1 large egg
dash of soy sauce
1 tsp sunflower oil

Preparation and cooking time: 55 minutes

Each serving provides

kcal 502, protein 32 g, fat 9 g (of which saturated fat 2 g), carbohydrate 77 g (of which sugars 8 g), fibre 4 g

✓✓✓	A, B₁, B₆, B₁₂, E, niacin
✓✓	B₂, C, folate, selenium, zinc
✓	iron

1 Bring the stock to the boil in a large saucepan, add the rice and cook for 10–12 minutes or until the rice is just tender and most of the stock has been absorbed. Remove the pan from the heat, cover and set aside.

2 Heat a wok or large heavy-based frying pan until hot, then add the oil and swirl to coat the wok. Add the onion, garlic and carrots and stir-fry for 5 minutes or until the onion has softened.

3 Toss the pork into the wok and stir-fry for 3 minutes, then add the mushrooms and cook for 2 minutes. Add the chilli powder and turmeric and stir for a minute or two, then add the peas, ketchup and soy sauce.

4 Gradually add the cooked rice to the wok, tossing to mix, and stir-fry until all the ingredients are well blended and heated through. Toss in the spring onions and then the prawns. Remove from the heat and keep hot.

5 To make the omelette, beat the egg in a small bowl with the soy sauce and 1 tbsp water. Heat the oil in an 18 cm (7 in) omelette pan, pour in the egg mixture and fry until just set. Tip the omelette out onto a board, roll it up and cut into strips.

6 To serve, spoon the pork and rice mixture into a warmed serving dish and arrange the omelette strips on top.

Another idea

● Make beef nasi goreng using strips of lean rump steak, trimmed of fat, instead of pork. In step 2, stir-fry 1 seeded and diced large red pepper and 1 seeded and sliced fresh red chilli with the onion and garlic (omit the carrots). In step 3, stir in 1 tsp anchovy paste when adding the peas, ketchup and soy sauce. Replace the prawns with 4 finely shredded cabbage leaves.

Plus points

● This is a low-fat dish with 60% of the calories coming from carbohydrate – mainly supplied by the rice. Starchy carbohydrates are the best foods for energy as they break down slowly to offer a long-term energy source.
● Both prawns and pork are useful sources of selenium, an important micronutrient (needed in very small amounts). Selenium works to protect the cardiovascular system.

special meat

Wild boar ragù with soft polenta

Wild boar is a favourite throughout Tuscany and Umbria. Here it is cooked with lots of garlic, herbs and spices to make a wonderful thick sauce (ragù) for polenta. Serve with a rocket and radicchio salad – their slight bitterness is a great foil for the rich polenta and meat sauce – or with lightly braised greens.

Serves 4

450 g (1 lb) boneless wild boar for stewing, trimmed of fat and cut into bite-sized chunks

2 onions

1 cinnamon stick

250 ml (8½ fl oz) full-bodied red wine

15 juniper berries, lightly crushed

4 bay leaves

4 garlic cloves, thinly sliced

1 tbsp extra virgin olive oil

1 carrot, chopped

1 celery stick, chopped

1 can chopped tomatoes, about 400 g

1 tsp balsamic vinegar

300 ml (10 fl oz) beef stock, preferably home-made (see page 27)

10 g (¼ oz) dried porcini mushrooms, rinsed to remove any grit

a few sprigs of fresh herbs (rosemary, sage, oregano or parsley), leaves coarsely chopped

salt and pepper

Ricotta and rosemary polenta

300 g (10½ oz) instant polenta

100 g (3½ oz) ricotta cheese

1 tbsp finely chopped fresh rosemary

Preparation and cooking time: 2¾ hours, plus up to 2 days marinating

1 Place the wild boar in a bowl. Chop one of the onions and add it to the bowl with the cinnamon stick, wine, juniper berries, bay leaves, garlic, and pepper to taste. Cover and marinate in the fridge overnight, or up to 2 days.

2 Remove the meat from the marinade and pat dry with kitchen paper. Strain the marinade and set aside. Chop the remaining onion. Heat the oil in a flameproof casserole, add the meat and brown lightly on all sides. Add the chopped onion, carrot and celery and cook for 3–4 minutes or until the vegetables soften a little.

3 Add the marinade, the tomatoes with their juice, the vinegar, stock, mushrooms and herbs. Season to taste. Bring to the boil, then cover and simmer for about 2 hours or until the meat is tender. Remove from the heat and keep hot while you cook the polenta.

4 Cook the polenta according to the packet instructions until it is smooth and thick. Beat in the ricotta cheese and rosemary, and continue stirring over a low heat until the ricotta is absorbed.

5 Divide the polenta among 4 warmed plates and spoon the wild boar and sauce over. Serve immediately.

Plus points

● Wild boar is a very tasty, rich meat, so a little goes a long way. It is also very lean. Like pork, it is an excellent source of vitamin B_{12}, which is essential for healthy red blood cells.

● Polenta is a gluten-free source of starchy carbohydrate. It also provides some potassium.

● Adding ricotta cheese to the polenta does not increase the overall fat content of this dish as much as you would think because ricotta is relatively low in fat compared with most other cheeses. It is also a good source of calcium and vitamins B_2 and B_{12}.

Each serving provides

kcal 533, **protein** 39 g, **fat** 13 g (of which saturated fat 4 g), **carbohydrate** 66 g (of which sugars 9 g), **fibre** 3 g

✓✓✓	A, B_1, B_6, B_{12}, C, E, niacin
✓✓	B_2, iron, potassium, zinc
✓	calcium

special meat

Some more ideas

- Use 250 g (8½ oz) boneless lean pork leg steaks instead of the wild boar. About 45 minutes before the end of the cooking time, cut 200 g (7 oz) pork or venison sausages into bite-sized pieces and fry them in a non-stick frying pan, without any fat, until browned on all

sides. Remove with a draining spoon and drain on kitchen paper, then add to the pork and cook for a further 30 minutes.

- Make the ragù with wild boar sausages. Sauté the chopped onion, carrot and celery with 4 coarsely chopped garlic cloves. Add 400 g (14 oz) wild boar sausages, skinned and broken

into small pieces, and sauté until they are browned, breaking them up into little bits. Add 250 ml (8½ fl oz) full-bodied red wine with the tomatoes, stock, mushrooms and herbs (omit the vinegar) and simmer for 30 minutes.

- Serve the ragù with noodles or pasta rather than with polenta.

Spanish rabbit and chickpea stew

In Spain, the home of this spicy dish, chickpeas are very popular and are often stewed with a small amount of meat and a vegetable or two to make hearty one-pot feasts. Serve this with chunks of rustic sourdough bread on the side, so that you can dip it in to enjoy every drop of the delicious gravy.

Serves 4

2 tbsp extra virgin olive oil

340 g (12 oz) boneless rabbit, cut into large chunks

2 onions, roughly chopped

3 garlic cloves, chopped

1 large red pepper, seeded and roughly chopped

1 tbsp paprika, preferably smoked

½ tsp mild chilli powder

½ tsp ground cumin

large pinch of ground cinnamon

2 bay leaves

250 ml (8½ fl oz) dry white wine

250 ml (8½ fl oz) chicken stock

1 can chopped tomatoes, about 225 g

2 tbsp tomato purée

3 tbsp chopped fresh flat-leaf parsley

2 pinches of saffron threads

4 tbsp hot water

1 can chickpeas, about 400 g, drained and rinsed

225 g (8 oz) new potatoes, scrubbed and halved

2 sprigs of fresh oregano or marjoram, leaves coarsely chopped

grated zest and juice of 1 small orange, preferably a blood orange

salt and pepper

Preparation time: 20 minutes
Cooking time: about 1½ hours

1 Heat the oil in a flameproof casserole, add the chunks of rabbit and sauté until browned on all sides. Add the onions, garlic and red pepper and fry, stirring frequently, for 5 minutes or until the onions are softened. Add the paprika, chilli powder, cumin, cinnamon and bay leaves, stir well and fry for 1 minute.

2 Add the wine, stock, tomatoes with their juice, tomato purée and half of the parsley. Cover and bring to the boil, then reduce the heat to very low and simmer for about 40 minutes or until the rabbit is very tender. Meanwhile, crumble the saffron into a small bowl and add the hot water. Stir, then leave to soak for 15–20 minutes.

3 Add the chickpeas and potatoes to the stew, together with the saffron and its soaking water, the oregano or marjoram, and orange zest and juice. Stir, then simmer for 25–30 minutes or until the gravy has thickened and is not too soupy. Taste and add seasoning if needed, and remove the bay leaves if you prefer. Serve hot, sprinkled with the remaining parsley.

Another idea

- Instead of rabbit, use lean pork fillet (tenderloin) or lamb fillet or boneless leg, trimmed of fat and cut into bite-sized chunks.

Plus points

- Chickpeas are an important source of vegetable protein in many parts of the world, and they are a good source of dietary fibre. Surprisingly, in this recipe the chickpeas provide a greater amount of iron per portion than the rabbit (1.5 mg compared to 0.9 mg). The absorption of the iron is helped by the generous amounts of vitamin C provided by the vegetables, in particular red pepper.
- Rabbit is an excellent low-fat source of protein. It can be substituted for chicken breast in many recipes because its pale-coloured meat looks and tastes quite similar. Nutritionally, it contains twice as much iron as chicken breast.

Each serving provides

kcal 417, **protein** 33 g, **fat** 15 g (of which saturated fat 3 g), **carbohydrate** 41 g (of which sugars 14 g), fibre 9 g

✓✓✓	A, B_1, B_6, B_{12}, C, E, niacin
✓✓	B_2, folate, iron, selenium, zinc

Indian lamb with spiced lentils

Freshly ground spices make this dhansak-style curry fabulously fragrant, while green lentils give texture and substance. Serve with chapattis and yogurt, and saffron rice sprinkled with chopped, toasted cashews.

Serves 4

6 black peppercorns

1 tbsp cumin seeds

seeds from 8 cardamom pods

2 tbsp sunflower oil

1 large onion, sliced

2 garlic cloves, crushed

5 cm (2 in) piece fresh root ginger, finely chopped

1 fresh red chilli, seeded and finely chopped

1 cinnamon stick

1 tsp turmeric

450 g (1 lb) lean boneless leg of lamb or neck fillet, trimmed of fat and cut into cubes

600 ml (1 pint) hot lamb stock, preferably home-made (see page 27)

225 g (8 oz) green lentils

4 plum tomatoes, quartered

juice of ½ lemon

2 tbsp chopped fresh coriander

salt and pepper

Preparation time: 30 minutes

Cooking time: about 1½ hours

Each serving provides

kcal 500, **protein** 43 g, **fat** 23 g (of which saturated fat 8 g), **carbohydrate** 34 g (of which sugars 5 g), **fibre** 7 g

✓✓✓	B₁, B₆, B₁₂, E, niacin, iron, selenium, zinc
✓✓	B₂, potassium
✓	A, calcium

1 Crush the peppercorns with the cumin and cardamom seeds in a pestle and mortar or an electric grinder. Set aside.

2 Heat the oil in a large flameproof casserole, add the onion and fry gently for 5 minutes or until softened. Add the garlic, ginger and chilli and fry for a further 3 minutes, then add the crushed spices and the cinnamon stick and turmeric. Fry gently for 30 seconds, stirring constantly.

3 Add the lamb and stir to coat with the spices. Fry gently for about 4 minutes or until the meat is browned all over. Gradually pour in the stock, stirring well, and bring to the boil. Reduce the heat, cover and cook gently for 1 hour or until the lamb is almost cooked and tender.

4 Meanwhile, rinse and drain the lentils, then place them in a saucepan and cover with fresh cold water. Bring to the boil. Boil uncovered for 15 minutes. Drain.

5 Add the lentils and tomatoes to the curry and cook for 15–20 minutes or until the lamb and lentils are tender. Stir in the lemon juice and fresh coriander and season with salt and pepper to taste. Serve hot.

Some more ideas

• If it's more convenient, you can cook the curry in the oven. In step 3, after bringing to the boil, cover the casserole and place it in a preheated 180°C (350°F, gas mark 4) oven. Cook for 1¼ hours. Add the lentils and tomatoes and cook for a further 20 minutes or until tender.

• Ethnic grocers and health food shops sell a wide range of lentils. Any of them can be used, but check first whether they are best soaked before cooking, because you may need to plan ahead. Red split lentils (masoor dhal) and split peas are a good choice because they do not need soaking.

• If you've no fresh tomatoes, use 1 can chopped tomatoes, about 225 g, with the juice.

Plus points

• Lentils are an excellent source of dietary fibre and a good source of iron, as well as a useful source of vitamins B₁ and B₆. In addition, an average portion normally provides almost 100% of the adult RNI for selenium (this can vary according to the soil in which the plant is grown).

Thai beef noodle soup

**Bursting with flavour, this main-course beef soup is packed with vegetables and noodles.
You can eat the noodles, beef and vegetables with chopsticks, then enjoy the soup with a spoon.**

Serves 4

15 g (½ oz) dried shiitake mushrooms

100 ml (3½ fl oz) boiling water

1 litre (1¾ pints) beef stock, preferably
    home-made (see page 27)

4 fresh lime leaves, torn

1 lemongrass stalk, cut into 3 pieces

1 garlic clove, crushed

1 fresh red chilli, seeded and chopped

2.5 cm (1 in) piece fresh root ginger, grated

15 g (½ oz) fresh coriander

150 g (5½ oz) carrot

100 g (3½ oz) leek

2 celery sticks, about 100 g (3½ oz) in total

100 g (3½ oz) sugarsnap peas

100 g (3½ oz) Chinese leaves

340 g (12 oz) lean rump steak, trimmed of fat

100 ml (3½ fl oz) low-fat coconut milk

3 sheets dried medium Chinese egg noodles,
    about 260 g (9 oz) in total

finely grated zest and juice of 1 lime

4 tsp fish sauce, or to taste

Preparation and cooking time: about 50 minutes

Each serving provides

kcal 357, **protein** 23 g, **fat** 7 g (of which
saturated fat 3 g), **carbohydrate** 25 g (of
which sugars 7 g), **fibre** 3 g

✓✓✓	A, B₁, B₆, B₁₂, C, E, niacin
✓✓	B₂, zinc
✓	calcium, iron

1 Put the mushrooms into a small bowl, add the boiling water and leave to soak for 20 minutes.

2 Meanwhile, pour the stock into a large saucepan and add the lime leaves, lemongrass, garlic, chilli and ginger. Separate the coriander leaves from the stalks and set the leaves aside. Chop the stalks and add them to the stock. Cover the pan and bring the stock just to the boil, then reduce the heat to very low. Let the stock simmer gently for 10 minutes while you prepare the vegetables and beef.

3 Drain the mushrooms, pouring the soaking liquid into the simmering stock. Cut each mushroom in half lengthways. Chop the carrot, leek and celery into fine strips about 5 cm (2 in) long. Slice the sugarsnap peas in half lengthways, and finely shred the Chinese leaves. Slice the beef into thin strips about 1 cm (½ in) wide.

4 Remove the lemongrass and lime leaves from the stock. Bring the stock back to the boil, then add the carrot, leek and celery. Cover and simmer for 3 minutes. Pour in the coconut milk and increase the heat. Just as the liquid comes to the boil, add the noodles, crushing them in your hands as you drop them into the pan. Stir in the mushrooms and beef, bring back to a simmer and cook, uncovered, for 1 minute. Stir well, then add the sugarsnap peas and Chinese leaves. Simmer for a further 3 minutes or until the beef, noodles and vegetables are just tender. Add the lime zest and juice and the fish sauce and stir well. Taste and add more fish sauce if you like.

5 To serve, transfer the noodles, beef and vegetables to bowls using a draining spoon. Ladle the coconut stock over, sprinkle with the coriander leaves and serve immediately.

Plus points

• Celery provides potasssium, a mineral that is important for the regulation of fluid balance in the body, thus helping to prevent high blood pressure.

• Coconut milk is a typical ingredient of Thai cooking. The low-fat version (88% fat-free) has 12 g fat per 100 g (3½ oz) compared with 17 g in ordinary full-fat coconut milk.

• Sugarsnap peas are a good source of soluble fibre and vitamin C.

special meat

Some more ideas

• Instead of dried mushrooms, use 50 g (1¾ oz) sliced button mushrooms and add an extra 100 ml (3½ fl oz) stock.

• If you can't get fresh lime leaves, use 8 dried lime leaves. Remove the dry stalks and discard them, then crush the leaves before using.

• Low-fat coconut milk is available in cans in most supermarkets, but if you can't find it use half the quantity of ordinary coconut milk.

• This soup is also delicious made with chicken. Simmer 900 ml (1½ pints) chicken stock with the Thai flavourings, then add the carrot strips and 100 g (3½ oz) baby corn, quartered lengthways (omit the leek and celery). Simmer for 5 minutes. Add 4 skinless boneless chicken thighs, about 340 g (12 oz) in total, cut into strips, the soaked shiitake mushrooms and their liquid and 50 g (1¾ oz) chopped spring onions. Stir well, then cover and simmer for about 3 minutes. Add the coconut milk and 1 vacuum pack of ready-cooked Chinese noodles, about 150 g (5½ oz), the sugarsnap peas and Chinese leaves. Stir again and simmer for 3 minutes or until the chicken is cooked and the vegetables are tender. Finish with the lime zest and juice, fish sauce and coriander leaves.

special meat

Lamb with peppers and macaroni

This Italian-style casserole is ideal for a special family dinner – it can be put in the oven well in advance, leaving time to do other things. Don't worry if you get delayed, as the lamb improves with longer cooking. Or it can be left to stand and reheated, with the macaroni added at the last minute. Serve with ciabatta.

Serves 4

1 tbsp extra virgin olive oil

500 g (1 lb 2 oz) lean lamb neck fillet, trimmed of fat and sliced

250 g (8½ oz) shallots, halved or quartered

1 carrot, cut into large dice

2 celery sticks, thickly sliced

2 red peppers, seeded and cut into large dice

2 garlic cloves, chopped

1 can chopped tomatoes, about 400 g

200 ml (7 fl oz) dry white wine

juice of 1 lemon

3 bay leaves

2 tsp light soft brown sugar

340 g (12 oz) macaroni

salt and pepper

To garnish

grated zest of 1 lemon

4 tbsp chopped parsley

Preparation time: 25 minutes

Cooking time: 1½ hours

Each serving provides

kcal 655, **protein** 38 g, **fat** 22 g (of which saturated fat 9 g), **carbohydrate** 81 g (of which sugars 17 g), **fibre** 7 g

✓✓✓	A, B$_1$, B$_6$, B$_{12}$, C, E, folate, niacin, zinc
✓✓	B$_2$, iron, selenium
✓	potassium

1 Preheat the oven to 180°C (350°F, gas mark 4). Heat the oil in a large flameproof casserole, add the slices of lamb and fry over a high heat for 5 minutes or until evenly browned, turning the pieces several times.

2 Add the shallots, carrot, celery, red peppers and garlic and fry for 3–4 minutes or until softened. Add the tomatoes with their juice, the wine, lemon juice, bay leaves and sugar, and season to taste. Stir well and bring to the boil, then stir again. Cover the casserole with its lid, transfer it to the oven and cook for 1¼ hours or until the lamb is tender.

3 When the lamb is nearly done, drop the pasta into a large saucepan of boiling water. When the water returns to the boil, cook for 10–12 minutes, or according to the packet instructions, until al dente. Drain and stir into the lamb, then taste for seasoning. Serve hot, garnished with grated lemon zest and chopped parsley.

Some more ideas

● Diced lean boneless leg of lamb or trimmed shoulder can be used instead of neck fillet.

● For a Greek lamb and pasta casserole, fry 500 g (1 lb 2 oz) minced lamb with 1 sliced onion in a non-stick frying pan, without any fat. Drain in a sieve so that fat from the lamb can be discarded, then put the meat and onion in a large saucepan. Add 2 tsp crushed coriander seeds and 2 chopped garlic cloves and cook for 1 minute, then stir in 200 ml (7 fl oz) dry white wine, 300 ml (10 fl oz) lamb or vegetable stock, 2 tbsp tomato purée and salt and pepper to taste. Cover and simmer for 30 minutes, stirring occasionally. Add the juice of 1 lemon with the cooked macaroni, then taste for seasoning. Top with 200 g (7 oz) cooked shelled broad beans tossed with 2 tbsp each chopped fresh mint and parsley.

● Other pasta shapes such as fusilli (spirals) or conchiglie (shells) can be used.

Plus points

● Red peppers are an excellent source of vitamin C – weight for weight they contain over twice as much as oranges. They also provide good amounts of carotenoids and bioflavonoids – both antioxidants that help to protect against heart disease and cancer.

● When vegetables are cooked in a casserole they take on the flavour of the sauce, so it is a good way to encourage children to eat them. For very fussy children, scoop out the meat with a draining spoon and disguise the vegetables by puréeing them with the sauce.

Toulouse sausages with Puy lentils and golden mash

This easy recipe turns just a few simple ingredients into the most satisfying and well-balanced midweek supper. Serve with thickly sliced crusty bread and a peppery rocket or watercress salad.

Serves 4

170 g (6 oz) Puy lentils

750 ml (1¼ pints) chicken stock

1 large onion, roughly chopped

600 g (1 lb 5 oz) potatoes, peeled and quartered

300 g (10½ oz) butternut squash, peeled, seeded and chopped

4 Toulouse sausages, about 280 g (10 oz) in total

1 can chopped tomatoes, about 400 g

3 tbsp semi-skimmed milk

salt and pepper

To serve

4 tsp balsamic vinegar

3 tbsp chopped fresh flat-leaf parsley

Preparation and cooking time: about 1 hour

Each serving provides

kcal 520, **protein** 23 g, **fat** 18 g (of which saturated fat 7 g), **carbohydrate** 67 g (of which sugars 11 g), **fibre** 9 g

✓✓✓ A, B$_1$, B$_6$, C, E, folate, niacin, iron

✓✓ selenium, zinc

✓ B$_{12}$

1 Preheat the grill. Rinse the lentils and place them in a saucepan with 600 ml (1 pint) of the stock and the chopped onion. Bring to the boil, then reduce the heat, cover and simmer for 25 minutes.

2 Meanwhile, cook the potatoes in a large saucepan of boiling water for 10 minutes. Add the butternut squash and continue cooking for 10 minutes or until both the squash and potatoes are tender.

3 While the lentils, potatoes and squash are cooking, grill the sausages for 15 minutes, turning them several times so they brown evenly.

4 Slice the sausages thickly and add them to the lentils, together with the tomatoes and their juice. If the lentils have absorbed all the liquid, add the remaining stock. Cover and cook for a further 10 minutes.

5 Drain the potatoes and squash and mash them with the milk. Season with salt and pepper to taste. Spoon onto plates and top with the sausages and lentils. Drizzle over the vinegar and sprinkle with the chopped parsley. Serve immediately.

Some more ideas

• For an oven-baked version, soften 1 large roughly chopped onion in 1 tbsp extra virgin olive oil in a flameproof casserole. Stir in 2 chopped garlic cloves and 1 large seeded and chopped fresh red chilli. Cook for 2 minutes, then stir in 1 seeded and chopped red pepper, 450 g (1 lb) potatoes, peeled and cut into large dice, 170 g (6 oz) Puy lentils, 1 can chopped tomatoes, about 400 g, with the juice, and 750 ml (1¼ pints) chicken stock. Add 200 g (7 oz) sliced smoked pork boiling sausage or a combination of sliced kabanos sausage and pork boiling sausage. Season well and bring to the boil, then cover and transfer to a preheated 180ºC (350ºF, gas mark 4) oven. Cook for 1 hour. Stir in 2 tbsp chopped parsley before serving.

• Turn this into a vegetarian dish by using vegetarian sausages and vegetable stock.

• Use kabocha squash instead of butternut.

Plus points

• Mashing the potatoes with butternut squash adds wonderful colour and texture, as well as beneficial nutrients. Butternut squash is an excellent source of vitamin C and a useful source of vitamin E and beta-carotene.

special meat

144

Veal escalopes with herbs

In this light summery dish, ultra-thin and tender veal escalopes are in and out of the pan in less than 5 minutes, after which the pan is quickly deglazed with wine to make a sauce and fresh herbs are added to pep up the flavour. New potatoes and spinach are excellent accompaniments.

Serves 4

900 g (2 lb) baby new potatoes, scrubbed

4 veal escalopes, about 140 g (5 oz) each, beaten to 5 mm (¼ in) thickness

2 tbsp plain flour

2 tbsp extra virgin olive oil

45 g (1½ oz) unsalted butter

400 g (14 oz) baby leaf spinach

grated zest and juice of 1 lemon

75 ml (2½ fl oz) dry white wine

4 tbsp chopped mixed fresh herbs, such as parsley, chervil, chives and tarragon

salt and pepper

To serve

lemon wedges

Preparation and cooking time: about 45 minutes

Each serving provides

kcal 494, **protein** 39 g, **fat** 19 g (of which saturated fat 8 g), **carbohydrate** 42 g (of which sugars 5 g), **fibre** 5 g

✓✓✓ A, B$_1$, B$_6$, B$_{12}$, E, folate, niacin, zinc

✓✓ B$_2$, calcium, iron, selenium

1 First cook the potatoes. Place them in a large saucepan of boiling water and boil for 15 minutes or until tender.

2 Meanwhile, pat the escalopes dry with kitchen paper. Season the flour with a little salt and pepper, then toss the escalopes in the flour to coat them lightly and evenly all over. Shake off any excess flour.

3 Heat half of the oil in a large non-stick frying pan over a moderate heat. Add half of the butter and heat until it starts to foam, then add the escalopes. Fry for 2–3 minutes on each side or until the juices run clear and not pink when the meat is pierced with a skewer or fork. You may need to cook the meat in 2 batches. Remove the escalopes from the pan with a draining spoon, place on a warmed serving dish and keep hot.

4 Drain the potatoes in a colander. Add the remaining 1 tbsp oil to the hot saucepan in which you cooked the potatoes and set over a low heat. Add the potatoes and toss gently until they are coated with oil. Add the spinach to the pan in 4 batches, gently tossing and stirring so that it wilts in the heat from the potatoes. Add the lemon juice, and season with salt and pepper to taste. Stir gently to mix. Cover and keep warm while you make the sauce.

5 Return the frying pan to the heat and add the wine. Increase the heat so the liquid bubbles, then stir vigorously to dislodge any bits of sediment in the pan. Boil for 1 minute or until reduced and syrupy, then season lightly. Remove the pan from the heat and add the rest of the butter. Stir until it has melted.

6 Scatter the mixed herbs over the escalopes, then drizzle with the wine sauce. Sprinkle the lemon zest over the potatoes and spinach. Serve the vegetables alongside the escalopes, with lemon wedges for squeezing.

Plus points

● This dish is especially rich in B vitamins. There is B$_6$ in the veal and the new potatoes, B$_3$ and B$_{12}$ in the veal. The veal, spinach and new potatoes together provide an excellent source of folate.

● New potatoes in their skins and lemon juice are both good sources of vitamin C, which may help to reduce the severity of the common cold.

special meat

Some more ideas

- Lean pork or turkey escalopes, beaten thin, can be cooked in the same way. Remove them from the pan and keep hot. Add 2 seeded and thinly sliced green peppers and 250 g (8½ oz) sliced button mushrooms to the juices in the pan. Stir and toss over a high heat for 2 minutes, then add 1 crushed garlic clove and the white wine. Cook until the liquid is reduced and syrupy. Season with salt and pepper to taste. Pour the wine sauce over the escalopes (omit the mixed herbs) and serve with boiled new potatoes in their skins.

- Replace the spinach with 250 g (8½ oz) thinly sliced okra. Cook the potatoes, then drain. Heat the oil in the hot pan, add the okra and lemon juice and cook, stirring frequently, for 4 minutes. Add the potatoes, season with salt and pepper to taste and toss gently over a low heat until combined. Sprinkle with the lemon zest before serving.

Shabu-shabu steak

This Japanese-style one-pot meal is great fun as a sociable dinner party dish, but it is also simple enough to serve as a midweek meal. Meat and vegetables are cooked briefly in stock, then the delicious stock is served as a soup at the end of the meal, so maximum vitamins and minerals from the ingredients are retained.

Serves 4

400 g (14 oz) lean rump steak, trimmed of fat

10 cm (4 in) piece white radish (mooli or daikon)

200 g (7 oz) shiitake or chestnut mushrooms, sliced

200 g (7 oz) pak choi, sliced

8 spring onions, finely shredded

200 g (7 oz) bean sprouts

300 g (10½ oz) fine Chinese egg noodles

1 tsp toasted sesame oil

1.2 litres (2 pints) vegetable stock

2 tbsp fish sauce

Chilli dipping sauce

8 tbsp shoyu (Japanese soy sauce)

2 tbsp lemon juice

2 tbsp chilli sauce, or to taste

2 spring onions, finely chopped

Preparation time: 50–60 minutes, including 50 minutes part freezing

Cooking time: 1–1½ minutes each batch

Each serving provides

kcal 502, **protein** 38 g, **fat** 12 g (of which saturated fat 4 g), **carbohydrate** 65 g (of which sugars 7 g), **fibre** 5 g

✓✓✓	B₁, B₂, B₆, B₁₂, C, E, folate, niacin
✓✓	selenium
✓	A

1 Wrap the beef in cling film and place the package flat in the freezer for 50 minutes or until partially frozen.

2 Meanwhile, peel the white radish and cut it across into thin slices, then cut into 2.5 cm (1 in) diamonds or triangles. Arrange with the mushrooms, pak choy, spring onions and bean sprouts on 4 individual plates. Cover with cling film and chill until required.

3 Cook the noodles in a saucepan of boiling water for 3 minutes, or cook or soak them according to the packet instructions. Drain, toss in the sesame oil and add to the plates.

4 Remove the beef from the freezer and cut it across the grain into wafer-thin slices. Arrange on the plates next to the vegetables. Keep covered and chilled until ready to serve. Mix the ingredients for the dipping sauce and pour into 4 small serving bowls. Set aside.

5 To serve, heat the stock until boiling, then add the fish sauce. Pour into a meat fondue pot or Mongolian fire pot set over a flame in the centre of the table and keep at a steady simmer. Let each person put a few mushroom slices, radish, spring onions, bean sprouts and slices of meat into the stock and cook for 30–60 seconds, then add some pak choy and noodles and cook for a further 30 seconds. Use a draining spoon to transfer the noodles, meat and vegetables to individual serving bowls. Mouthfuls held on chopsticks can be dipped into the sauce.

6 Continue in this way until all the ingredients have been cooked, then ladle the stock into the serving bowls. Season to taste with any remaining dipping sauce and drink as a soup.

Some more ideas

• For a Japanese chicken 'fondue', use thinly sliced skinless boneless chicken breasts (fillets) in place of the beef. Cook for 1 minute before adding the vegetables.

• For a milder dipping sauce, mix together 3 tbsp mirin (sweetened Japanese rice wine), 3 tbsp lemon juice, 120 ml (4 fl oz) rice vinegar and 4 tbsp shoyu.

Plus points

• Pak choy, a leafy green Oriental cabbage, is a good source of vitamin C. The amount in this recipe provides per portion 31% of the recommended daily amount of vitamin C for an adult woman.

special meat

Persian lamb couscous

Chunks of lean lamb are gently simmered with dates in a richly spiced gravy, then piled atop couscous and pistachio nuts, and sprinkled with pomegranate seeds. Serve this exotic dish for a special family meal or a make-ahead dish for entertaining, accompanied by some Arabic flat bread and a simple leafy green salad.

Serves 4

340 g (12 oz) boneless lean leg of lamb, trimmed of fat and cut into cubes

1 tbsp extra virgin olive oil

4 garlic cloves, finely chopped

2 tbsp finely chopped fresh root ginger

2 onions, halved and thinly sliced

1 fresh red chilli, seeded and thinly sliced

2 pinches of saffron threads

2 tsp ground coriander

2 tsp ground cumin

1 tsp ground cinnamon

1 tsp paprika

100 g (3½ oz) stoned dates, sliced

600 ml (1 pint) lamb stock, preferably home-made (see page 27)

salt and pepper

seeds of 1 small pomegranate to garnish

Pistachio couscous

300 ml (10 fl oz) lamb stock, preferably home-made (see page 27)

400 g (14 oz) couscous

15 g (½ oz) fresh coriander, chopped

25 g (scant 1 oz) pistachio nuts, roughly chopped

Preparation time: 20 minutes
Cooking time: about 1¼ hours

1 Heat a large non-stick saucepan and fry the cubes of lamb, in batches, until browned all over. Lift from the pan with a draining spoon and set aside.

2 Add the oil to the pan, then add the garlic, ginger, onions and chilli. Fry, stirring frequently, over a low heat for 10 minutes.

3 Return the lamb to the pan, together with the saffron, ground coriander, cumin, cinnamon and paprika. Cook for about 30 seconds, stirring well, then add the dates and stock. Season to taste. Cover and simmer gently for 1 hour or until the lamb is tender.

4 About 15 minutes before the lamb is ready, prepare the couscous. Heat the stock until boiling, then add the couscous and return to the boil. Remove from the heat, cover tightly and set aside to soak for 10 minutes.

5 Fork the couscous through lightly to fluff up the grains, then toss in the coriander and pistachios and pile onto a warmed large serving platter. Spoon the lamb on top of the couscous, sprinkle with the pomegranate seeds and serve immediately.

Some more ideas

- If you want to get ahead, you can cook this dish up to the end of step 3 the day before, then let it cool and keep it in a covered bowl in the fridge. When you are ready to serve, reheat the lamb while the couscous is soaking in step 4, making sure it is piping hot and bubbling.
- For a more peppery flavour, instead of coriander toss chopped rocket or watercress with the couscous.

Plus points

- Pomegranate seeds make a very pretty garnish for sweet or savoury dishes, and they are deliciously sweet and tart all at once. In addition they contribute vitamin C and fibre, so all the more reason for using them often.

Each serving provides

kcal 561, **protein** 35 g, **fat** 15 g (of which saturated fat 4 g), **carbohydrate** 76 g (of which sugars 22 g), **fibre** 3 g

✓✓✓	B_1, B_6, B_{12}, E, niacin, iron
✓✓	B_2, C, zinc
✓	A, folate

Pork medallions with peppers

This quick sauté makes an excellent dinner party dish, with its well-balanced sweet and sour elements coming from balsamic vinegar, oranges and olives. It is especially good – and extra nutritious – served with broccoli.

Serves 4

340 g (12 oz) mixed basmati and wild rice

600 ml (1 pint) boiling water

2 oranges

1 tbsp extra virgin olive oil

340 g (12 oz) pork fillet (tenderloin), sliced across into medallions 1 cm (½ in) thick

1 large sweet onion, e.g. Vidalia, Spanish or red, halved lengthways and thinly sliced into half rings

1 red pepper, seeded and sliced into strips

1 yellow pepper, seeded and sliced into strips

1 large carrot, grated

1 garlic clove, finely chopped

90 ml (3 fl oz) orange juice

3 tbsp balsamic vinegar

30 g (1 oz) stoned black olives, chopped or sliced

30 g (1 oz) fresh basil leaves

salt and pepper

Preparation and cooking time: about 50 minutes

Each serving provides

kcal 539, protein 27 g, fat 8 g (of which saturated fat 2 g), carbohydrate 89 g (of which sugars 19 g), fibre 5 g

✓✓✓ A, B$_1$, B$_6$, B$_{12}$, niacin

✓✓ B$_2$, folate

✓ iron, potassium, selenium, zinc

1 Put the rice in a saucepan and pour over the boiling water. Bring back to the boil, then reduce the heat to low. Cover and simmer for about 15 minutes, or according to the packet instructions, until the rice is tender and all the water has been absorbed.

2 Meanwhile, peel the oranges and cut them crossways into slices about 1 cm (½ in) thick. Stack the slices 3 or 4 at a time and cut into quarters. (If possible, use a chopping board with a well to catch the juices.) Set the orange slices and juice aside.

3 Heat the oil in a large non-stick frying pan over a moderately high heat. Cook the pork medallions, in batches, for 2–3 minutes on each side. Remove the meat with a draining spoon and set aside.

4 Reduce the heat to moderate and add the onion, pepper strips, carrot and garlic to the pan. Cover and cook, stirring frequently, for 5–6 minutes or until the vegetables start to soften. Add 2 tbsp water, then the measured orange juice and the balsamic vinegar. Stir well to mix. Cover and cook for 3–4 minutes or until the vegetables are tender.

5 Return the pork to the pan. Add the olives, orange slices and their juice and the basil leaves. Cook for 1 minute to reheat the pork, stirring well. Taste and add salt and pepper, if needed.

6 To serve, divide the rice among 4 warmed plates and place the pork medallions and vegetables on top. Drizzle over any juices remaining in the pan and serve immediately.

Another idea

• For lamb with peppers and Puy lentils, use lean lamb neck fillets or boneless lean lamb leg steaks, beaten thin, instead of pork fillet, and substitute 250 g (8½ oz) Puy lentils, cooked according to the packet instructions, for the rice. Omit the basil and flavour the lamb with ½ tsp chopped fresh rosemary.

Plus points

• Wild rice comes from North America. It is not a true rice, but the seeds of a wild aquatic grass. It is gluten-free, like the basmati rice it is mixed with here, and contains useful amounts of B vitamins, particularly niacin, as well as dietary fibre.

special meat

152

Venison and mushroom terrine

Lean venison makes a great terrine. Mixing it with pork and then marinating the meats in port and spices will give it extra flavour and add moisture. Serve the terrine sliced with a mixed salad and wholemeal or Granary bread for a delicious lunch, or use it in sandwiches. It can also be served as a starter for 8.

Serves 4

450 g (1 lb) minced venison

200 g (7 oz) lean minced pork

1 tsp finely grated fresh root ginger

12 juniper berries, crushed

½ tsp freshly grated nutmeg

¼ tsp ground cloves

100 ml (3½ fl oz) port

2 tbsp extra virgin olive oil

100 g (3½ oz) button or chestnut mushrooms, finely chopped

1 egg, beaten

4 tbsp chopped parsley

2 tsp fresh thyme leaves

salt and pepper

Preparation time: 30 minutes, plus 2 hours marinating and chilling to set

Cooking time: 1¼–1½ hours

Each serving provides

kcal 300, **protein** 39 g, **fat** 12 g (of which saturated fat 3 g), **carbohydrate** 3 g (of which sugars 3 g), **fibre** 0 g

✓✓✓	B₁, B₆, E, niacin
✓✓	B₁₂, C, zinc
✓	A, folate, iron

1 Mix the venison with the pork, ginger, juniper berries, nutmeg and cloves. Sprinkle over the port and half of the oil and mix in. Cover and leave to marinate for about 2 hours.

2 Meanwhile, heat the remaining 1 tbsp oil in a non-stick frying pan, add the mushrooms and fry, stirring, for about 5 minutes or until they are brown and quite dry. Set aside to cool.

3 Preheat the oven to 180°C (350°F, gas mark 4). Line the bottom and sides of a 1.2 litre (2 pint) terrine dish or loaf tin with non-stick baking parchment or greaseproof paper.

4 Stir the mushrooms, egg, parsley and thyme into the meat mixture and season with salt and pepper. Spoon into the lined terrine or tin and smooth the surface, then cover with a double layer of foil, tightly sealing the edges. Bake for 1¼–1½ hours. Lift the foil and test that it is cooked by checking that the juices run clear when a skewer is inserted in the middle.

5 Remove the foil. Put a double layer of parchment or greaseproof paper over the top of the terrine or tin, then lay 2 cans, end to end, or other weights on top. Juices will ooze out and set to a jelly. Refrigerate until cold and set, overnight if possible. Return the terrine to room temperature before serving.

Plus points

• Venison contains more iron than beef and provides valuable amounts of zinc. It is also particularly low in fat, with only 1.6 g fat for every 100 g (3½ oz), compared to 4.1 g fat in the same weight of rump steak.

• Traditional meat terrines are made moist and juicy with pork back fat or belly of pork, which makes them high in saturated fat. Lean minced pork is used here instead. It adds flavour and succulence, but contains only 5 g fat per 100 g (3½ oz) meat.

• In Asian cultures mushrooms are renowned for their ability to boost the immune system, and the Chinese have put them to medicinal use for over 6000 years.

special meat

Some more ideas

• Use red wine instead of port for the marinade and cook 1 crushed large garlic clove with the mushrooms in step 2. Instead of the ginger, juniper, nutmeg and cloves, add 1 tbsp paprika with the herbs. Spoon half of the mixture into the tin and arrange 12 whole stuffed green olives in 2 rows down the centre. Spoon the rest of the mixture on top and smooth it down, then cook as in the main recipe. When the terrine is sliced, each slice will show a cross section of olive.

• For a stronger mushroom flavour, soak 15 g (½ oz) dried porcini mushrooms to rehydrate, then chop and fry with the fresh mushrooms in step 2.

• Add 6 chopped ready-to-eat prunes with the mushrooms in step 4.

• If you like, before serving garnish the terrine with a salsa-style topping of finely chopped tomato, red onion and parsley.

A glossary of nutritional terms

Antioxidants These are compounds that help to protect the body's cells against the damaging effects of free radicals. Vitamins C and E, beta-carotene (the plant form of vitamin A) and the mineral selenium, together with many of the phytochemicals found in fruit and vegetables, all act as antioxidants.

Calorie A unit used to measure the energy value of food and the intake and use of energy by the body. The scientific definition of 1 calorie is the amount of heat required to raise the temperature of 1 gram of water by 1 degree Centigrade. This is such a small amount that in this country we tend to use the term kilocalories (abbreviated to *kcal*), which is equivalent to 1000 calories. Energy values can also be measured in kilojoules (kJ): 1 kcal = 4.2 kJ.

A person's energy (calorie) requirement varies depending on his or her age, sex and level of activity. The estimated average daily energy requirements are:

Age (years)	Female (kcal)	Male (kcal)
1–3	1165	1230
4–6	1545	1715
7–10	1740	1970
11–14	1845	2220
15–18	2110	2755
19–49	1940	2550
50–59	1900	2550
60–64	1900	2380
65–74	1900	2330

Carbohydrates These energy-providing substances are present in varying amounts in different foods and are found in three main forms: sugars, starches and non-starch polysaccharides (NSP), usually called fibre.

There are two types of sugars: *intrinsic sugars*, which occur naturally in fruit (fructose) and sweet-tasting vegetables, and *extrinsic sugars*, which include lactose (from milk) and all the non-milk extrinsic sugars (NMEs) – sucrose (table sugar), honey, treacle, molasses and so on. The NMEs, or 'added' sugars, provide only calories, whereas foods containing intrinsic sugars also offer vitamins, minerals and fibre. Added sugars (*simple carbohydrates*) are digested and absorbed rapidly to provide energy very quickly. Starches and fibre (*complex carbohydrates*), on the other hand, break down more slowly to offer a longer-term energy source (see also Glycaemic Index). Starchy carbohydrates are found in bread, pasta, rice, wholegrain and breakfast cereals, and potatoes and other starchy vegetables such as parsnips, sweet potatoes and yams.

Healthy eating guidelines recommend that at least half of our daily energy (calories) should come from carbohydrates, and that most of this should be from complex carbohydrates. No more than 11% of our total calorie intake should come from 'added' sugars. For an average woman aged 19–49 years, this would mean a total carbohydrate intake of 259 g per day, of which 202 g should be from starch and intrinsic sugars and no more than 57 g from added sugars. For a man of the same age, total carbohydrates each day should be about 340 g (265 g from starch and intrinsic sugars and 75 g from added sugars).

See also Fibre and Glycogen.

Cholesterol There are two types of cholesterol – the soft waxy substance called blood cholesterol, which is an integral part of human cell membranes, and dietary cholesterol, which is contained in food. *Blood cholesterol* is important in the formation of some hormones and it aids digestion. High blood cholesterol levels are known to be an important risk factor for coronary heart disease, but most of the cholesterol in our blood is made by the liver – only about 25% comes from cholesterol in food. So while it would seem that the amount of cholesterol-rich foods in the diet would have a direct effect on blood cholesterol levels, in fact the best way to reduce blood cholesterol is to eat less saturated fat and to increase intake of foods containing soluble fibre.

Fat Although a small amount of fat is essential for good health, most people consume far too much. Healthy eating guidelines recommend that no more than 33% of our daily energy intake (calories) should come from fat. Each gram of fat contains 9 kcal, more than twice as many calories as carbohydrate or protein, so for a woman aged 19–49 years this means a daily maximum of 71 g fat, and for a man in the same age range 93.5 g fat.

Fats can be divided into 3 main groups: saturated, monounsaturated and polyunsaturated, depending on the chemical structure of the fatty acids they contain. *Saturated fatty acids* are found mainly in animal fats such as butter and other dairy products and in fatty meat. A high intake of saturated fat is known to be a risk factor for coronary heart disease and certain types of cancer. Current guidelines are that no more than 10% of our daily calories should come from saturated fats, which is about 21.5 g for an adult woman and 28.5 g for a man.

Where saturated fats tend to be solid at room temperature, the *unsaturated fatty acids* –

monounsaturated and polyunsaturated – tend to be liquid. *Monounsaturated fats* are found predominantly in olive oil, groundnut (peanut) oil, rapeseed oil and avocados. Foods high in *polyunsaturates* include most vegetable oils – the exceptions are palm oil and coconut oil, both of which are saturated.

Both saturated and monounsaturated fatty acids can be made by the body, but certain polyunsaturated fatty acids – known as *essential fatty acids* – must be supplied by food. There are 2 'families' of these essential fatty acids: *omega-6*, derived from linoleic acid, and *omega-3*, from linolenic acid. The main food sources of the omega-6 family are vegetable oils such as olive and sunflower; omega-3 fatty acids are provided by oily fish, nuts, and vegetable oils such as soya and rapeseed.

When vegetable oils are hydrogenated (hardened) to make margarine and reduced-fat spreads, their unsaturated fatty acids can be changed into trans fatty acids, or 'trans fats'. These artificially produced trans fats are believed to act in the same way as saturated fats within the body – with the same risks to health. Current healthy eating guidelines suggest that no more than 2% of our daily calories should come from trans fats, which is about 4.3 g for an adult woman and 5.6 g for a man. In thinking about the amount of trans fats you consume, remember that major sources are processed foods such as biscuits, pies, cakes and crisps.

Fibre Technically non-starch polysaccharides (NSP), fibre is the term commonly used to describe several different compounds, such as pectin, hemicellulose, lignin and gums, which are found in the cell walls of all plants. The body cannot digest fibre, nor does it have much nutritional value, but it plays an important role in helping us to stay healthy.

Fibre can be divided into 2 groups – soluble and insoluble. Both types are provided by most plant foods, but some foods are particularly good sources of one type or the other. *Soluble fibre* (in oats, pulses, fruit and vegetables) can help to reduce high blood cholesterol levels and to control blood sugar levels by slowing down the absorption of sugar. *Insoluble fibre* (in wholegrain cereals, pulses, fruit and vegetables) increases stool bulk and speeds the passage of waste material through the body. In this way it helps to prevent constipation, haemorrhoids and diverticular disease, and may protect against bowel cancer.

Our current intake of fibre is around 12 g a day. Healthy eating guidelines suggest that we need to increase this amount to 18 g a day.

Free radicals These highly reactive molecules can cause damage to cell walls and DNA (the genetic material found within cells). They are believed to be involved in the development of heart disease, some cancers and premature ageing. Free radicals are produced naturally by the body in the course of everyday life, but certain factors, such as cigarette smoke, pollution and over-exposure to sunlight, can accelerate their production.

Gluten A protein found in wheat and, to a lesser degree, in rye, barley and oats, but not in corn (maize) or rice. People with *coeliac disease* have a sensitivity to gluten and need to eliminate all gluten-containing foods, such as bread, pasta, cakes and biscuits, from their diet.

Glycaemic Index (GI) This is used to measure the rate at which carbohydrate foods are digested and converted into sugar (glucose) to raise blood sugar levels and provide energy. Foods with a high GI are quickly broken down and offer an immediate energy fix, while those with a lower GI are absorbed more slowly, making you feel full for longer and helping to keep blood sugar levels constant. High-GI foods include table sugar, honey, mashed potatoes and watermelon. Low-GI foods include pulses, wholewheat cereals, apples, cherries, dried apricots, pasta and oats.

Glycogen This is one of the 2 forms in which energy from carbohydrates is made available for use by the body (the other is *glucose*). Whereas glucose is converted quickly from carbohydrates and made available in the blood for a fast energy fix, glycogen is stored in the liver and muscles to fuel longer-term energy needs. When the body has used up its immediate supply of glucose, the stored glycogen is broken down into glucose to continue supplying energy.

Minerals These inorganic substances perform a wide range of vital functions in the body. The *macrominerals* – calcium, chloride, magnesium, potassium, phosphorus and sodium – are needed in relatively large quantities, whereas much smaller amounts are required of the remainder, called *microminerals*. Some microminerals (selenium, magnesium and iodine, for example) are needed in such tiny amounts that they are known as *'trace elements'*.

There are important differences in the body's ability to absorb minerals from different foods, and this can be affected by the presence of other substances. For example, oxalic acid, present in spinach, interferes with the absorption of much of the iron and calcium spinach contains.
• *Calcium* is essential for the development of strong bones and teeth. It also plays an important role in blood clotting. Good sources include dairy products, canned fish (eaten with their bones) and dark green, leafy vegetables.
• *Chloride* helps to maintain the body's fluid balance. The main source in the diet is table salt.
• *Chromium* is important in the regulation of blood sugar levels, as well as levels of fat and cholesterol in the blood. Good dietary sources include red meat, liver, eggs, seafood, cheese and wholegrain cereals.

• *Copper*, component of many enzymes, is needed for bone growth and the formation of connective tissue. It helps the body to absorb iron from food. Good sources include offal, shellfish, mushrooms, cocoa, nuts and seeds.
• *Iodine* is an important component of the thyroid hormones, which govern the rate and efficiency at which food is converted into energy. Good sources include seafood, seaweed and vegetables (depending on the iodine content of the soil in which they are grown).
• *Iron* is an essential component of haemoglobin, the pigment in red blood cells that carries oxygen around the body. Good sources are offal, red meat, dried apricots and prunes, and iron-fortified breakfast cereals.
• *Magnesium* is important for healthy bones, the release of energy from food, and nerve and muscle function. Good sources include wholegrain cereals, peas and other green vegetables, pulses, dried fruit and nuts.
• *Manganese* is a vital component of several enzymes that are involved in energy production and many other functions. Good dietary sources include nuts, cereals, brown rice, pulses and wholemeal bread.
• *Molybdenum* is an essential component of several enzymes, including those involved in the production of DNA. Good sources are offal, yeast, pulses, wholegrain cereals and green leafy vegetables.
• *Phosphorus* is important for healthy bones and teeth and for the release of energy from foods. It is found in most foods. Particularly good sources include dairy products, red meat, poultry, fish and eggs.
• *Potassium*, along with sodium, is important in maintaining fluid balance and regulating blood pressure, and is essential for the transmission of nerve impulses. Good sources include fruit, especially bananas and citrus fruits, nuts, seeds, potatoes and pulses.
• *Selenium* is a powerful antioxidant that protects cells against damage by free radicals. Good dietary sources are meat, fish, dairy foods, brazil nuts, avocados and lentils.
• *Sodium* works with potassium to regulate fluid balance, and is essential for nerve and muscle function. Only a little sodium is needed – we tend to get too much in our diet. The main source in the diet is table salt, as well as salty processed foods and ready-prepared foods.
• *Sulphur* is a component of 2 essential amino acids. Protein foods are the main source.
• *Zinc* is vital for normal growth, as well as reproduction and immunity. Good dietary sources include oysters, red meat, peanuts and sunflower seeds.

Phytochemicals These biologically active compounds, found in most plant foods, are believed to be beneficial in disease prevention. There are literally thousands of different phytochemicals, amongst which are the following:

• *Allicin*, a phytochemical found in garlic, onions, leeks, chives and shallots, is believed to help lower high blood cholesterol levels and stimulate the immune system.
• *Bioflavonoids*, of which there are at least 6000, are found mainly in fruit and sweet-tasting vegetables. Different bioflavonoids have different roles – some are antioxidants, while others act as anti-disease agents. A sub-group of these phytochemicals, called *flavonols*, includes the antioxidant *quercetin*, which is believed to reduce the risk of heart disease and help to protect against cataracts. Quercetin is found in tea, red wine, grapes and broad beans.
• *Carotenoids*, the best known of which are *beta-carotene* and *lycopene*, are powerful antioxidants thought to help protect us against certain types of cancer. Highly coloured fruits and vegetables, such as blackcurrants, mangoes, tomatoes, carrots, sweet potatoes, pumpkin and dark green, leafy vegetables, are excellent sources of carotenoids.
• *Coumarins* are believed to help protect against cancer by inhibiting the formation of tumours. Oranges are a rich source.
• *Glucosinolates*, found mainly in cruciferous vegetables, particularly broccoli, Brussels sprouts, cabbage, kale and cauliflower, are believed to have strong anti-cancer effects. *Sulphoraphane* is one of the powerful cancer-fighting substances produced by glucosinolates.
• *Phytoestrogens* have a chemical structure similar to the female hormone oestrogen, and they are believed to help protect against hormone-related cancers such as breast and prostate cancer. One of the types of these phytochemicals, called *isoflavones*, may also help to relieve symptoms associated with the menopause. Soya beans and chickpeas are a particularly rich source of isoflavones.

Protein This nutrient, necessary for growth and development, for maintenance and repair of cells, and for the production of enzymes, antibodies and hormones, is essential to keep the body working efficiently. Protein is made up of *amino acids*, which are compounds containing the 4 elements that are necessary for life: carbon, hydrogen, oxygen and nitrogen. We need all of the 20 amino acids commonly found in plant and animal proteins. The human body can make 12 of these, but the remaining 8 – called *essential amino acids* – must be obtained from the food we eat.

Protein comes in a wide variety of foods. Meat, fish, dairy products, eggs and soya beans contain all of the essential amino acids, and are therefore called first-class protein foods. Pulses, nuts, seeds and cereals are also good sources of protein, but do not contain the full range of essential amino acids. In practical terms, this really doesn't matter – as long as you include a variety of different protein foods in your diet, your body will get all the amino acids it needs. It is important, though, to eat protein foods every day because the essential amino acids cannot be stored in the body for later use.

The RNI of protein for women aged 19–49 years is 45 g per day and for men of the same age 55 g. In the UK most people eat more protein than they need, although this isn't normally a problem.

Reference Nutrient Intake (RNI) This denotes the average daily amount of vitamins and minerals thought to be sufficient to meet the nutritional needs of almost all individuals within the population. The figures, published by the Department of Health, vary depending on age, sex and specific nutritional needs such as pregnancy. RNIs are equivalent to what used to be called Recommended Daily Amounts or Allowances (RDA).

RNIs for adults (19–49 years)

Vitamin A	600–700 mcg
Vitamin B_1	0.8 mg for women, 1 mg for men
Vitamin B_2	1.1 mg for women, 1.3 mg for men
Niacin	13 mg for women, 17 mg for men
Vitamin B_6	1.2 mg for women, 1.4 mg for men
Vitamin B_{12}	1.5 mg
Folate	200 mcg (400 mcg for first trimester of pregnancy)
Vitamin C	40 mg
Vitamin E	no recommendation in the UK; the EC RDA is 10 mg, which has been used in all recipe analyses in this book
Calcium	700 mg
Chloride	2500 mg
Copper	1.2 mg
Iodine	140 mcg
Iron	14.8 mg for women, 8.7 mg for men
Magnesium	270–300 mg
Phosphorus	550 mg
Potassium	3500 mg
Selenium	60 mcg for women, 75 mcg for men
Sodium	1600 mg
Zinc	7 mg for women, 9.5 mg for men

Vitamins These are organic compounds that are essential for good health. Although they are required in only small amounts, each one has specific vital functions to perform. Most vitamins cannot be made by the human body, and therefore must be obtained from the diet. The body is capable of storing some vitamins (A, D, E, K and B_{12}), but the rest need to be provided by the diet on a regular basis. A well-balanced diet, containing a wide variety of different foods, is the best way to ensure that you get all the vitamins you need.

Vitamins can be divided into 2 groups: *water-soluble* (B complex and C) and *fat-soluble* (A, D, E and K). Water-soluble vitamins are easily destroyed during processing, storage, and the preparation and cooking of food. The fat-soluble vitamins are less vulnerable to losses during cooking and processing.

• *Vitamin A* (retinol) is essential for healthy vision, eyes, skin and growth. Good sources include dairy products, offal (especially liver), eggs and oily fish. Vitamin A can also be obtained from *beta-carotene*, the pigment found in highly coloured fruit and vegetables. In addition to acting as a source of vitamin A, beta-carotene has an important role to play as an antioxidant in its own right.

• *The B Complex vitamins* have very similar roles to play in nutrition, and many of them occur together in the same foods.

Vitamin B_1 (thiamin) is essential in the release of energy from carbohydrates. Good sources include milk, offal, meat (especially pork), wholegrain and fortified breakfast cereals, nuts and pulses, yeast extract and wheat germ. White flour and bread are fortified with B_1 in the UK.

Vitamin B_2 (riboflavin) is vital for growth, healthy skin and eyes, and the release of energy from food. Good sources include milk, meat, offal, eggs, cheese, fortified breakfast cereals, yeast extract and green leafy vegetables.

Niacin (nicotinic acid), sometimes called vitamin B_3, plays an important role in the release of energy within the cells. Unlike the other B vitamins it can be made by the body from the essential amino acid tryptophan. Good sources include meat, offal, fish, fortified breakfast cereals and pulses. White flour and bread are fortified with niacin in the UK.

Pantothenic acid, sometimes called vitamin B_5, is involved in a number of metabolic reactions, including energy production. This vitamin is present in most foods; notable exceptions are fat, oil and sugar. Good sources include liver, kidneys, yeast, egg yolks, fish roe, wheat germ, nuts, pulses and fresh vegetables.

Vitamin B_6 (pyridoxine) helps the body to utilise protein and contributes to the formation of haemoglobin for red blood cells. B_6 is found in a wide range of foods including meat, liver, fish, eggs, wholegrain cereals, some vegetables, pulses, brown rice, nuts and yeast extract.

Vitamin B_{12} (cyanocobalamin) is vital for growth, the formation of red blood cells and maintenance of a healthy nervous system. B_{12} is unique in that it is principally found in foods of animal origin. Vegetarians who eat dairy products will get enough, but vegans need to ensure they include food fortified with B_{12} in their diet. Good sources of B_{12} include liver, kidneys, oily fish, meat, cheese, eggs and milk.

Folate (folic acid) is involved in the manufacture of amino acids and in the production of red blood cells. Recent research suggests that folate may also help to protect against heart disease. Good sources of folate are green leafy vegetables, liver, pulses, eggs, wholegrain cereal products and fortified breakfast cereals, brewers' yeast, wheatgerm, nuts and fruit, especially grapefruit and oranges.

Biotin is needed for various metabolic reactions and the release of energy from foods. Good sources include liver, oily fish, brewers' yeast, kidneys, egg yolks and brown rice.

• *Vitamin C* (ascorbic acid) is essential for growth and vital for the formation of collagen (a protein needed for healthy bones, teeth, gums, blood capillaries and all connective tissue). It plays an important role in the healing of wounds and fractures, and acts as a powerful antioxidant. Vitamin C is found mainly in fruit and vegetables.

• *Vitamin D* (cholecalciferol) is essential for growth and the absorption of calcium, and thus for the formation of healthy bones. It is also involved in maintaining a healthy nervous system. The amount of vitamin D occurring naturally in foods is small, and it is found in very few foods – good sources are oily fish (and fish liver oil supplements), eggs and liver, as well as breakfast cereals, margarine and full-fat milk that are fortified with vitamin D. Most vitamin D, however, does not come from the diet but is made by the body when the skin is exposed to sunlight.

• *Vitamin E* is not one vitamin, but a number of related compounds called tocopherols that function as antioxidants. Good sources of vitamin E are vegetable oils, polyunsaturated margarines, wheatgerm, sunflower seeds, nuts, oily fish, eggs, wholegrain cereals, avocados and spinach.

• *Vitamin K* is essential for the production of several proteins, including prothombin which is involved in the clotting of blood. It has been found to exist in 3 forms, one of which is obtained from food while the other 2 are made by the bacteria in the intestine. Vitamin K_1, which is the form found in food, is present in broccoli, cabbage, spinach, milk, margarine, vegetable oils, particularly soya oil, cereals, liver, alfalfa and kelp.

Nutritional analyses

The nutritional analysis of each recipe has been carried out using data from *The Composition of Foods* with additional data from food manufacturers where appropriate. Because the level and availability of different nutrients can vary, depending on factors like growing conditions and breed of animal, the figures are intended as an approximate guide only.

The analyses include vitamins A, B_1, B_2, B_6, B_{12}, niacin, folate, C, D and E and the minerals calcium, copper, iron, potassium, selenium and zinc. Other vitamins and minerals are not included, as deficiencies are rare. Optional ingredients and optional serving suggestions have not been included in the calculations.

glossary

158

Index

*Printing and binding: Tien Wah Press Limited, Singapore
Separations: Colour Systems Ltd, London
Paper: StoraEnso*

Book code: 400-201-01
ISBN: 0 276 42888 9
Oracle Code: 250000565S

index